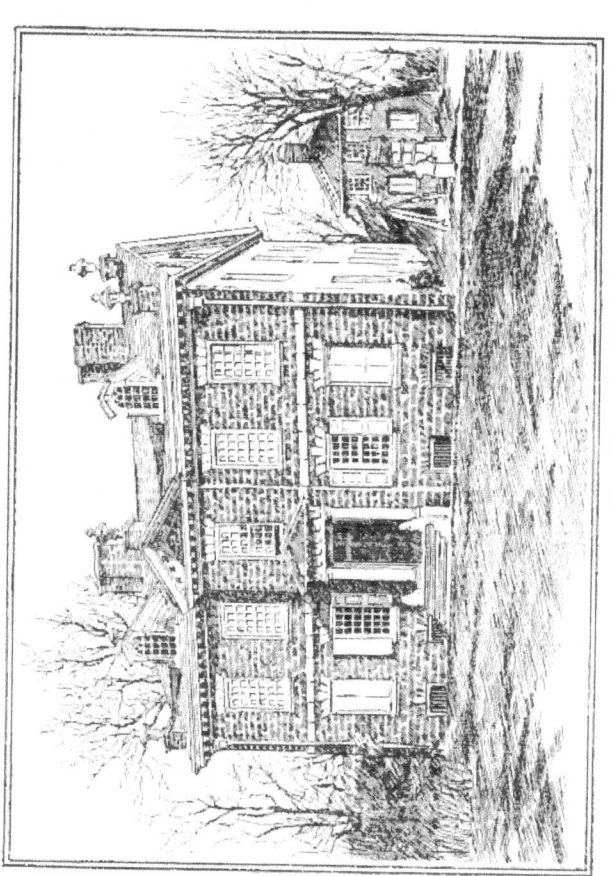

Chew House

THE GUIDEBOOK TO HISTORIC GERMANTOWN
[PENNSYLVANIA]

Prepared for The Site & Relic Society
by
Charles F. Jenkins

HERITAGE BOOKS
2024

HERITAGE BOOKS

AN IMPRINT OF HERITAGE BOOKS, INC.

Books, CDs, and more—Worldwide

For our listing of thousands of titles see our website at
www.HeritageBooks.com

A Facsimile Reprint
Published 2024 by
HERITAGE BOOKS, INC.
Publishing Division
5810 Ruatan Street
Berwyn Heights, MD 20740

Originally published
Germantown, Pennsylvania
Site and Relic Society
Innes & Sons, Philadelphia
1902

— Publisher's Notice —
In reprints such as this, it is often not possible to remove blemishes from the original. We feel the contents of this book warrant its reissue despite these blemishes and hope you will agree and read it with pleasure.

International Standard Book Number
Paperbound: 978-0-7884-5129-4

CONTENTS

Chronology of Germantown	7
Bibliography of Germantown	9
Preface	11
How to Reach Germantown	15
The Settlement of Germantown	17
The Ancient Town	24
Main Street of Germantown	29
Excursion, East Side of Germantown	133
Excursion, West Side of Germantown	144
Short Account of Battle of Germantown	153
Francis Daniel Pastorius	162
Streets of Germantown	167
Index	173

LIST of ILLUSTRATIONS

Chew House,	2
Stenton,	19
Wagner House,	25
Thones Kunders' House,	31
Wister House,	39
Price Homestead. Ladies' Club House, Manheim,	47
Germantown Academy,	55
Carlton,	63
Morris House,	71
Market Square,	79
Spencer House. Home of Thomas Godfrey,	85
Green Tree Tavern,	91
Wyck,	95
Blair House,	101
Mennonite Meeting House,	107
Johnson House,	111
Grave Stone in Upper Burying Ground,	117
David Rittenhouse's Birthplace,	123
Ship House,	129
Hall of Chew House,	135
Billmyer House,	141
Parsonage of Dunkard Church,	149
Old Doors of Chew House.	157
George Hesser's House (Bayard House).	165

CHRONOLOGY OF GERMANTOWN

August	16, 1683,	Francis Daniel Pastorius reaches Philadelphia.
October	6, 1683,	Thirteen emigrants from Crefeld with their families reached Philadelphia.
October	12, 1683,	A Warrant was issued to Pastorius for land on behalf of the Germantown purchase.
October	24, 1683,	Thomas Fairman surveyed the land.
October	25, 1683,	Meeting in cave of Pastorius, where lots were drawn for the land and settlement was at once begun.
	1683,	First flour mill in Philadelphia County, erected near Germantown.
	1688,	Friends issue first public protest in America against human slavery.
	1690,	First paper mill in America erected in Germantown.
May	31, 1691,	Germantown incorporated.
	1705,	What is believed to be the first portrait in oil painted in America made in Germantown by Dr. Christopher Witt.
	1707,	Town loses its charter and is no longer incorporated.
	1708,	First Mennonite meeting house in America built in Germantown.
February	17, 1719,	Francis Daniel Pastorius died.
	1719,	Arrival in Germantown of the first body of Dunkards in America.
April	8, 1732,	David Rittenhouse born.
	1743,	First Bible in America, in an European language, printed in Germantown by Christopher Sauer.

HISTORIC GERMANTOWN

1760,	Germantown Academy founded.
1761,	Cliveden, the Chew House, built.
1764,	Sauer began the publication of the first religious magazine in America.
1764,	Invasion of Paxtang Boys.
1769,	Dr. Christopher Witt died.
1770,	First American book on Pedagogy published in Germantown.
1772–1773,	First type ever cast in America made in Germantown.
August 1–8, 1777,	Washington's army encamped near Germantown.
Sept. 12–14, 1777,	Washington's army returns to camp near Germantown.
September 25, 1777,	British army occupies Germantown.
October 4, 1777,	Battle of Germantown.
October 19, 1777,	British army leaves Germantown, moving into Philadelphia.
1793,	Yellow fever drives President Washington, members of his Cabinet and many citizens from Philadelphia to Germantown.
1794,	Washington spends two months in Germantown to escape heat of summer.
1798,	Yellow fever again fills Germantown with refugees from Philadelphia
February 12, 1801,	Germantown Turnpike incorporated.
July 20, 1825,	Lafayette visits Germantown.
June 6, 1832,	Steam railroad to Germantown opened.
1854,	Germantown ceases to be an independent borough and is made part of Philadelphia.

A PARTIAL BIBLIOGRAPHY OF GERMANTOWN

Those who may wish to learn more of the history of Germantown and its vicinity are referred to the following works:

The Settlement of Germantown,—by the Hon. Samuel W. Pennypacker, published by W. J. Campbell, 1899.

Watson's Annals, Volume II,—pages 16 to 72, and elsewhere.

Walks in Germantown,—by Townsend Ward, published in the Pennsylvania Magazine of History and Biography, beginning Vol. V, No. 1.

Germantown, Mount Airy and Chestnut Hill,—by the Rev. S. F. Hotchkin, published by P. W. Ziegler & Co., 1889.

History of Germantown Academy,—edited by Horace W. Smith, published 1882.

The German Pietists of Pennsylvania,—by Julius F. Sachse, published 1895.

The German Sectarians of Pennsylvania,—by Julius F. Sachse. Two volumes. Volume I, published 1889, covers 1708-1742. Volume II, published 1900, covers 1742-1800.

A History of the German Baptist Brethren (Dunkards),—by Martin G. Brumbaugh, Ph.D. Brethren Publishing House, Elgin, Ill., 1899,

The Old York Road and Its Early Associations,—1670-1870, by Mrs. Anne de B. Mears, published in Philadelphia, 1890, by Harper & Brother.

A Century of Germantown Methodism,—by Robert Thomas, published by Germantown Independent, 1895.

The Battle of Germantown,—by Dr. A. C. Lambdin, published in the Pennsylvania Magazine of History and Biography, Vol. I, No. 1.

The German Baptist Brethren or Dunkards,—by Rev. George N. Falkenstein.

History of the Mennonites,—by Daniel K. Cassel, Philadelphia, 1888.

In addition to this there are other articles in the *Pennsylvania Magazine* relating to Germantown, reference to which may be had by consulting the indices of the various volumes.

HISTORIC GERMANTOWN

The following genealogies relating to Germantown families contain some local historical information :

The Shoemaker Family,—by Thomas H. Shoemaker, Philadelphia, 1893.
History of the Bringhurst Family,—by Josiah Granville Leach, Philadelphia, 1901.
Genealogy of the Fisher Family,—by Anna Wharton Smith, Philadelphia, 1896.
Thones Kunders and His Children,—by Henry C. Conrad, Wilmington, Del.
Genealogy of the Roberdeau Family,—by Roberdeau Buchanan, 1876.
Christopher Sower and His Descendants, (chart),—by Charles S. Sower, 1887.
Genea-Biographical History of the Rittenhouse Family,—by Daniel K. Cassel, 1897.
The Levering Family,—by Colonel John Levering, 1897. (Wigard Levering, the immigrant, settled first in Germantown but removed to Roxborough).
The Keyser Family,—compiled by Charles S. Keyser, 1889.
History of the Cassel Family,—by Daniel K. Cassel, 1896.
Kulp Family History,—by Daniel K. Cassel, 1895.

The following works of fiction have more or less connection with Germantown :

Pemberton ; or, A Hundred Years Ago,—by Henry Peterson.
Hugh Wynne,—by Dr. S. Weir Mitchell.
The Legends of the American Revolution, 1776,—by George Lippard.
Washington and His Men,—by George Lippard.
The Passing of Thomas,—by Thomas A. Janvier.

PREFACE

FEW towns or cities of our country possess the historical associations of Colonial and Revolutionary times that attach to our suburb of Germantown. Its conception and settlement, the nationality and character of its early settlers, its architecture, its industrial life and enterprise (for it was the cradle of some of our greatest industries), all early gave it marked individuality. It was the threshold over which entered the great German immigration which brought many modifications in language, manners and religion to the commonwealth and nation. Germantown was the scene of a fierce conflict which had considerable influence on the destiny of the infant nation. It was the home, on two occasions, of the President of the United States and members of his cabinet, making it, to that extent, the seat of Government of the country. All these incidents and more make it an important spot in our country's history and growth.

Fortunately during the period which brought so many changes, and obliterated so many of the historical landmarks in all our old cities, Germantown slumbered quietly, off from the path of so-called progress and improvement and there are, consequently, left in it many landmarks of the last century.

HISTORIC GERMANTOWN

A complete history of Germantown is yet to be written. In no one place can be found a full and consecutive account of the settlement, rise and progress of the town. Hon. Samuel W. Pennypacker, in his "Settlement of Germantown," has covered with great thoroughness the causes which led to the German immigration and the settlement itself; Mr. Julius F. Sachse in his several histories of the German sects makes unnecessary any further research in this direction; the Rev. S. F. Hotchkin, in his "Germantown and Chestnut Hill," has brought together much valuable local information; Townsend Ward in his "Walks in Germantown," published in the Pennsylvania Magazine, Volumes V and VI, gives a wealth of local incident and tradition, but unfortunately he died before his labors were completed, his walks extending only to near the centre of the town. In "Watson's Annals" are many incidents of local history. Dr. Alfred C. Lambdin, in his admirable address on the "One Hundreth Anniversary of the Battle of Germantown," gives a full and comprehensive account of this important incident in the town's history, and in many other places are to be found scraps of historical material, but no one has as yet brought all together in a complete and harmonious whole.

This little book is not a history of Germantown. Its aim is to present in as brief a way as possible the main historic facts connected with the town and to arrange these facts in such a

HISTORIC GERMANTOWN

way that the sightseer may have no trouble in finding and identifying each particular site.

The thanks and indebtedness of the Society are due to Mr. Thomas H. Shoemaker, whose unequalled store of information and collection of photographs and prints of ancient Germantown has been largely drawn upon. Also to the Rev. Francis Heyl, to whose care was committed a portion of the work of writing; to Dr. Naaman H. Keyser, a life-long student of the town's history, whose collections of material have been freely placed at the disposal of the writer, and to General Louis Wagner, William E. Chapman, Esq., Rev. William Ashmead Schaeffer, Mr. Francis Howard Williams, Miss Anne H. Cresson, and others for valuable information.

Hail to posterity!
Hail, future men of Germanoplis!
Let the young generations yet to be
  Look kindly upon this.
Think how your fathers left their native land,—
Dear German-land! O sacred hearths and homes!—
  And, where the wild beast roams,
    In patience planned
New forrest-homes beyond the mighty sea,
  Then undisturbed and free
To live as brothers of one family.
  What pains and cares befell,
    What trials and what fears,
Remember, and wherein we have done well
Follow our footsteps, men of coming years!
  Where we have failed to do
    Aright, or wisely live,
Be warned by us, the better way pursue,
And, knowing we were human, even as you,
    Pity us and forgive!
    Farewell, Posterity!
    Farewell, dear Germany!
    Forevermore farewell!
                    JOHN G. WHITTIER.

From the Latin of Francis Daniel Pastorius in the Germantown Records. 1688.

HOW TO REACH GERMANTOWN

GERMANTOWN is reached by steam cars via the Pennsylvania Railroad from Broad Street Station and the Philadelphia and Reading Road from the Reading Terminal. The former road skirts the west of the town and the latter the east. On the Pennsylvania Railroad, Queen Lane Station is near the Manheim cricket grounds and makes a good starting point to visit the places described in the chapter, page 144. Chelten Avenue Station is near the centre of the town and nearest the Rittenhouse House and site of the first paper mill, while Upsal Station is nearest the Chew House. Wayne Junction Station, on the Reading Road, is located at the extreme lower end of the Main Street of Germantown and is a very good starting point for a sight-seeing tour. Chelten Avenue Station on the Reading Road will bring the tourist near the centre of the town.

Germantown may also be reached by the trolley cars on Eighth Street (take cars marked Chestnut Hill or Germantown) and by the Germantown trolley on Thirteenth Street. The Germantown and Chestnut Hill cars on Eighth Street traverse the Main Street, or the old and historic portion of the town, while the Thirteenth Street cars traverse Wayne

HISTORIC GERMANTOWN

Street (which is two long squares west of the Main Street) passing through the modern residence section. The trip out by trolley takes from fifty minutes to an hour. Fare, 5 cents.

The Reading Railroad to Germantown was the first railroad operated in Philadelphia. In 1827 Edward H. Bonsall and Joseph Leibert visited Mauch Chunk to see the great marvel, the gravity road. On their return they proceeded to awaken public interest in a railroad to Germantown. A charter was obtained and so eager were the public to invest that for every five shares subscribed three were allotted. John G. Watmough was elected President and Edward H. Bonsall, Treasurer.

The road was opened June 6th, 1832. The cars made six trips a day, drawn by horses. November 23d, following, the first locomotive, "Old Ironsides," probably the first made in the United States, made by Matthias W. Baldwin, the founder of the Baldwin locomotive works, was placed on the road. Crowds assembled at 9th and Green Streets, the Philadelphia Commons, to see the train pass. Farmers came long distances to see its arrival in Germantown. Almost every one is now familiar with the notice which stated that when it rained horses would draw the train, as the engine was not taken out in the wet. For an illustration and short account of "Old Ironsides" see Pennsylvania Magazine, Vol. XI, p. 80.

HISTORIC GERMANTOWN

THE SETTLEMENT OF GERMANTOWN

THE first settlers of Germantown came from the country of the lower Rhine, not far from the borders of Holland. The purchase of land was made through the Frankfort Company, of which Francis Daniel Pastorius was the agent in America for a number of years.

In 1683 thirteen families, including in all thirty-three persons, set out from Crefeld, their native town, for London, where passage had been engaged for them to Pennsylvania in the ship Concord, by James Claypole, a Quaker merchant of that city, who was to be their fellow passenger. On the 24th of July they sailed from London, and arrived in Philadelphia the 6th of October. They were met on landing by Pastorius who had preceded them a few weeks. On the 24th of October Thomas Fairman, the surveyor of the Province, laid out their land in the township, afterwards called Germantown, and on the next day the immigrants met in the cave of Pastorius on the bank of the Delaware and made selections of the plots

HISTORIC GERMANTOWN

of land by lot. Having done this, they proceeded at once to clear their land and erect dwellings before the winter should overtake them.

The following are the names of the thirteen settlers:

Abraham Op den Graeff,	Thones Kunders,
Herman Op den Graeff,	Reynier Tyson,
Lenart Arets,	Jan Lucken,
Jan Seimens,	Johannes Bleikers,
Willem Streypers,	Peter Keurlis,
Jan Lensen,	Abraham Tunes.
Dirck Op den Graeff,	

They were all Friends or Mennonites, but just how they were divided between these two bodies is not known. Before their departure from Germany there had been a Friends' Monthly Meeting held at Crefeld, which was discontinued immediately after their departure, indicating that all or nearly all the full body of members had gone. By 1690 when the village of Germantown had grown to forty-four families, twenty-eight of them were Friends and the other sixteen of other religious faiths.

The next year (1684) other immigrants arrived and thereafter a steady flow of settlers from Germany and the Rhine provinces came to Pennsylvania, the majority passing through

Stenton

HISTORIC GERMANTOWN

Germantown. Many remained in the town, among them the ancestors of some of our present day families,—the Keysers, Shoemakers, Johnsons, Rittenhouses, Leverings, Sauers, etc. Germantown was the threshold over which entered the new country the various German sects, the Dunkards, Lutherans, Swenkfelders, etc., now occupying the southeastern portion of Pennsylvania.

On the 13th of February, 1694, a number of Pietists, originally from Germany, embarked at London on the ship Sarah Maria for Pennsylvania. After many adventures the ship entered the Chesapeake and landed the immigrants in Maryland, whence they journeyed overland to Germantown. These men, with Johannes Kelpius, as their Superior, took up their residence on the Ridge, as the high land between the Wissahickon and Schuylkill is called. Here they built a tabernacle of logs. They spent their time mostly in seclusion, engaged in religious devotion, in the study of astronomy and the occult arts. These men gradually passed away, the Hermitage in Hermits' Lane, near the Wissahickon, being one of the few reminders of their existence.

The early settlers brought with them the habits of industry and thrift which characterize the German race. In addition to the cultivation of the soil, which was never their main dependence, they brought various trades with them. Many

HISTORIC GERMANTOWN

were linen weavers. In 1686 Abraham Op den Greaff petitioned the Council to grant him the Governor's premium for "The first and finest piece of linen cloth," and as early as 1692 Richard Fraeme wrote :

> "The Germantown of which I spoke before
> Which is at least in length one mile or more,
> Where lives High German people and Low Dutch
> Whose trade in weaving cloth is much,—
> Here grows the Flax as also you may know
> That from the same they do divide the tow."

Later the manufacture of stockings from the famous Germantown wool was begun and by 1760 the Rev. Andrew Burnaby writes :—"The Germantown thread stockings are in high estimation and the year before last I have been credibly informed there were manufactured in that town alone above 60,000 dozen pairs, their common retail price a dollar per pair."

"The earliest settlers used to make good linens and vend them in Philadelphia. They were also distinguished, even till modern times, for their fabric of Germantown stockings. This fact induced the Bank of Germantown to adopt a seal, with such a loom upon it. The linen sellers and weavers used to stand with the goods for sale on the edge of the pavement in Market Street, on the north side, near to Second street corner. The cheapness of imported stockings is now ruining their business."—*Watson's Annals.*

HISTORIC GERMANTOWN

The Borough of Germantown early adopted a label to mark their goods so that their excellent quality would be more easily recognized.

About this time the tanning industry had assumed considerable importance, as the following letter from John Morgan, Jr., dated at Reading, Pa., December 23, 1777, while Philadelphia was occupied by the British Army, shows :

"I understand that all the stocking weavers at Germantown with their looms and out of work supposed to be one hundred, also six or seven tanners who have large tan yards full of leather, part of which is nearly tanned ; they might easily be removed.

Query :—Are they not objects worthy of notice of Council ? Should the enemy determine to stay or leave Philadelphia this winter they will probably destroy them which would be a great loss to this State."

As has been pointed out elsewhere, the manufacture of paper was first begun in Germantown in 1690.

This pre-eminence in manufacturing, first encouraged by the character and skill of the early settlers and carried on by them in their homes, has continued to the present time, as the great number of factories and important manufacturing plants in the neighborhood testify.

THE ANCIENT TOWN

FOR many years Germantown consisted of a long, straggling village extending for nearly two miles along the Main Street. The appearance of the town was thoroughly German and continued so down through the period of the Revolution. The language of conversation among the inhabitants was mainly in German, until even a later period. The prevalence of yellow fever in Philadelphia in 1793 and again in later years caused many Philadelphians to take up their residence in Germantown, which made many changes in the language and customs of the town.

As originally laid out there were to be four distinct villages along the Main road, all within the limits of what is now Germantown.

Roughly their boundaries were: Germantown from the present Wayne Junction to the Abington Road, now Washington Lane, Cresheim from this point to about the Mermaid Tavern, Sommerhausen to about one-eighth of a mile above Chestnut Hill and Crefeldt to Streeper's Mill, which was where the turnpike crosses the Wissahickon at the foot of Chestnut Hill.

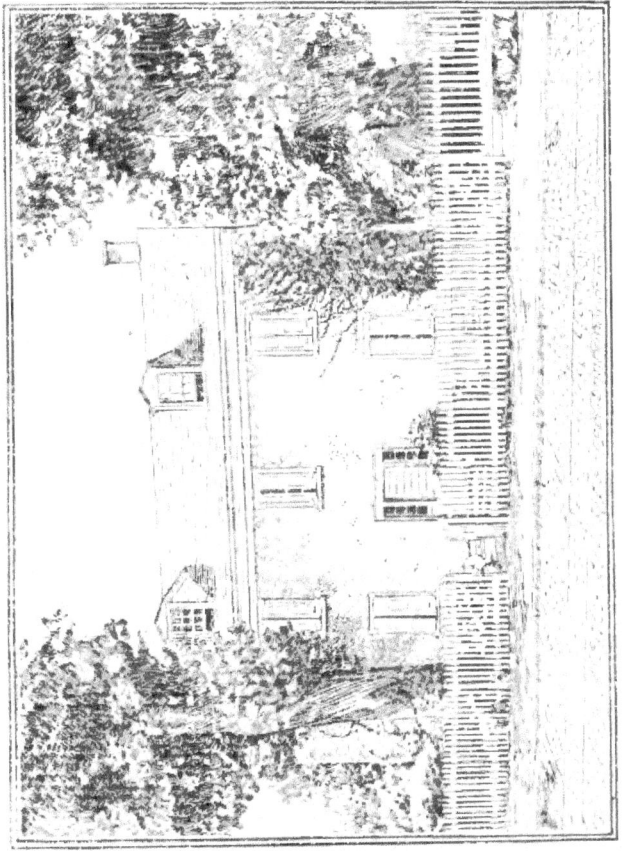

Wagner House, 4840 Main Street

HISTORIC GERMANTOWN

In later years the settlement above Upsal Street, surrounding the Dunkard Church, was called Beggarstown, for the origin of which name there are several theories. This name has, however, passed entirely away, but in the dispatches and descriptions of the Battle of Germantown, it is frequently used.

The early homes of the settle were first of logs and later of the rough, dark, native stone. Built with their gables in the road they had over-hanging hipped roofs and a projecting pent over the doorstep, as is still seen in the Engle house, No. 5938 Main Street; the door was divided in the middle to keep out stray animals, but with the upper portion open to admit air and light; on either side of the front door were little benches; the windows were small, usually swinging on hinges.

The sombre coloring of the houses, the solidity and air of comfort and thrift surrounding them, the rows of trees along the streets, the orchards and spacious farm buildings in the rear, are mentioned as prominent characteristics by many of the early travelers who have described the village.

As the tracts of land along the Main street were sold and divided up they usually retained their full depth so that the owners might have their wood and pasture lots in the rear with the house on the Main street. As more land was sold, these strips became still more narrow, so that at the time of

HISTORIC GERMANTOWN

the Revolution it was over and through these dividing walls and fences that the divisions of the American Army were compelled to advance, greatly retarding their progress and affording protection to the retreating British.

At the centre of the town was the market place and at the upper and lower ends were the two public burial grounds. On e east were several mills run by the waters of the Wingohocking, then a considerable stream, and on the west were even a greater number scattered along the Wissahickon. The cross roads of the town connected it with these mills and the ferry over the Schuylkill. The Abington Road, now Washington Lane, led to Abington Meeting. It was many years before any streets parallel with the Main street were opened.

About the middle of the eighteenth century, owing to the increase in wealth in Pennsylvania and particularly in Germantown and the coming to the town of wealthy Philadelphians who made their summer homes here, larger and better houses were built, of which the Dirck Keyser house, No. 6205 Main Street, is an example. There are yet many of these well built houses remaining and it is to arouse public sentiment to an appreciation of their artistic beauty, that they may be spared for many years as monuments of the early architecture, that the Site and Relic Society of Germantown has been formed.

HISTORIC GERMANTOWN

THE MAIN STREET

GERMANTOWN Avenue, Germantown Road, or the Great Road, as it was anciently called, is said to follow what was an old Indian trail. It is still quite crooked although it has been straightened some. As late as 1777, the year of the Battle, there were less than six cross roads. It therefore follows that what is of most historic interest is centered in the buildings along the Main Street, those on the cross streets being comparatively modern. But outlying at some distance, both on the east and west, there are historic points which come within the compass of what is now Germantown. It is proposed, as a matter of convenience, to take the visitor along the Main Street with very short side trips from it and then refer to the historic sites on each side of the town which can best be visited in separate expeditions.

Years ago the Germantown Road was called the worst road in the United States. The soil was of such a nature that in summer it was ground to fine, choking dust, while in winter and spring it was almost impassable on account of the mud for wheeled vehicles. The story is told of a gentleman who was

HISTORIC GERMANTOWN

building a house on the other side of the road from his home, and saddled his horse to ride across in safety. In 1800-1 the road was macadamized, forming part of the Germantown and Perkiomen Turnpike. The old toll house stood at Rittenhouse Street. Some of the mile stones erected by the Turnpike Company are still standing, one being at the corner of Main Street and Cliveden Avenue.

"Another great era of public benefit, now but little considered, was the formation of the Germantown turnpike—a measure got up chiefly through the exertions of Casper Haines. The common road through Germantown, before this time, at the breaking up of the winter, as well as at some other times, was impassable for wheel carriages. To that cause it was that most of the marketing, going through the place to Philadelphia, was all carried on horseback with side panniers and hampers, and the most of the horses were ridden by women. Think what a relief they have had since those days! It is a well known fact that horses and carriages have been swamped and lost! In going through the town, (now all well paved), their horses would enter the mud to their knees at every step, and not being able to progress faster than two or three miles an hour, and then often endangered. Now what a change do we witness! No men or women now on horseback with marketing, but going with easy spring dearborns at five and six miles an hour, as easy and safe as if in state carriages. Even wagon loads of hay can be seen sometimes passing in a trot!"

—*Watson's Annals.*

Thones Kunder's House, 5109 Main Street

HISTORIC GERMANTOWN

Starting at Wayne Junction, which we may well consider the southern boundry of the town, we should first make a short excursion to Stenton, four or five squares distant. The Pennsylvania Society of Colonial Dames has erected a sign post under the railroad bridge and one at each corner until Stenton is reached. The property is now in their charge and open at any time on application to the caretaker, but the best time to visit it is Saturday afternoons during May and June, and again in October, when the building is open and tea is served by the ladies of the Society to their guests. The house is partially furnished. The admission fee is 15 cents.

Stenton was erected by James Logan, for many years William Penn's able and faithful secretary, in 1727-34. The house is 55 feet front by 42 feet deep, with servants' quarters attached at the rear. From the cellar is an underground passageway leading to the stables, and some say, to the family burial ground beyond.

Stenton was occupied by General Washington on the evening of August 23, 1777, when the American Army was on its way to oppose Howe at Brandywine, and General Howe was quartered here later at the time of the Battle. Washington also dined with Dr. Logan, Sunday, July 8th, 1787, when he was attending the Constitutional Convention in Philadelphia.

HISTORIC GERMANTOWN

During the winter of British occupation an order was issued to burn all the mansions between Germantown and Philadelphia and seventeen were consumed at one time. Stenton is said to have been saved by the ready wit of the old colored woman left in charge. The two British dragoons who came to burn it went to the barn to get some straw to start the flames. While they were gone a British officer rode up looking for deserters. The old woman, in answer to his question, said she had seen two men who looked like deserters and that they had just gone to the barn. Just then the soldiers returned and despite their indignant protests and explanations the officer seized them and marched them off to the provost guard. Stenton was saved for the time and the efforts to burn it were not repeated.

Nos. 4518 and *4520 Main Street* is the old house of the Neglees. At the time of the Battle it was occupied by two sisters. As one of them was feeding the chickens she was startled by the noise of firearms. She quickly retired to the house and locked the windows and doors. After the battle two straggling "Red Coats" entered the house and asked for something to eat. When they left they took all they could carry with them. One of the soldiers asked "Had the army gone down yet?" to which one of the sisters replied: "Which

HISTORIC GERMANTOWN

army, the American or British?" This so angered the questioner that he drew his bayonet, and, rushing toward her, would have injured her had not her sister interfered. After the war the sister first named married John Harshey, a Hessian, who was captured by Washington at Trenton and who settled in this country, becoming a valued citizen.

The hill which starts at this point has been called Logan's Hill, but the common name is Neglee's Hill, from the Neglee family whose house appears nearby on a map of 1750.

The large house standing out on the brow of the hill, northwest corner of Apsley and Main Streets, was built in 1801 by Thomas Armat for his son. It is called "Loudoun" from that fact that Thomas Armat first settled in Loudoun County, Va. At the time of the Battle the wounded Americans were carried to the top of the hill on which the house stands, and later removed in wagons to the city. It is said many of the dead were buried here. The house is now occupied by the Logan family, descendants alike of James Logan, of Stenton, and Thomas Armat.

No. 4810 Main Street, is the Toland house, built about 1740. At the time of the Battle the house was the home of George Miller, an officer in the American army. On the night

HISTORIC GERMANTOWN

of the arrival of the British army in Germantown more than a dozen officers were quartered here. Jacob Miller, the son of George, related in later life his experience with them. Among other incidents one of the officers was taken ill, and Jacob, armed with a pass, was sent for assistance. At every little distance along the road he was challenged by a sentinel, but he got what was wanted and returned in safety. Jacob's mother was set to work baking bread for the officers. She was required to return in weight an amount equal to the flour she received, and as 100 pounds of flour will make about 130 pounds of bread, she had considerable flour left to pay her for her trouble.

No. 4817 Main Street has been called the Mehl house for the family that occupied it a hundred years ago. Some soldiers killed in the Battle are said to have been buried at the gateway.

No. 4825, the Ottinger house, was built in 1781 by Christopher Ottinger, a soldier of the Pennsylvania line, who volunteered at the age of 17. The walls are two feet thick, even the partition on the first floor being of stone. The rafters of the rear building are of unhewn trees.

Captain Douglas Ottinger, son of the above, the inventor of the Ottinger life car, was born here December 11th, 1804. In 1849 he equipped eight life-saving stations on the New Jersey

HISTORIC GERMANTOWN

coast with complete and effective life-saving apparatus. He was a captain in the U. S. Revenue Marine.

No. 4840 Main Street, called the Wagner house, was used as one of the main hospitals after the Battle. The big wooden doors of the stable in the rear were taken from their hinges and arranged as operating tables. The house belonged to Samuel Mechlin and his family, who left Germantown on the arrival of the British army. Mechlin was a tanner and everything of value about the house was seized, including a quantity of hides which were afterward recovered. The floors still show the blood stains of the wounded. Many died here and were buried in a trench in the rear. Seventy years ago some workmen in digging a post hole unearthed a number of relics which evidently had belonged to Hessian soldiers. The house was built in 1747.

No. 4908 Main Street is called the Henry house, having been in possession of that family for many years. The oldest portion was erected in 1760, but additions were made later. In 1828 it was bought by John S. Henry, the father of Alexander Henry, three times mayor of the city and member of Congress. The latter passed here the greater portion of his youth.

HISTORIC GERMANTOWN

Opposite the Henry house, occupying the northeast corner of East Logan Street and Main Street, is the Lower Germantown Burial Ground, sometimes called Hood's Burying Ground. Here are the remains of many of the early families of Germantown and their descendants. Note the quaint old gravestone built in the corner of the wall with its inscription, "Memendo Mory" and symbolic cross-bones. Also the stone some thirty feet from Main Street and ten from the north wall, erected by John F. Watson, the annalist, over the gaves of General Agnew and Colonel Bird, British officers, killed at the Battle of Germantown. Near the front gateway is the grave of Christian Frederick Post, a noted Moravian missionary to the Indians. The oldest stone in the yard is that of Joseph Coulston, 1707–8. Note also the stone with the inscription:

> " He was noble hearted & amiable &
> Intelligent, having been awarded
> A silver goblet for a literary
> Production at the age of 18."

The marble wall at the front was erected with money left for the purpose by William Hood, a resident of Germantown, who accumulated wealth and died in Paris in 1850.

The graveyard was presented to the borough of Germantown in 1693 by Jan Streepers.

Wister House, 5261 Main Street

HISTORIC GERMANTOWN

No. 5109 Main Street occupies the site of Thones Kunder's home, one of the original settlers of Germantown, and, so far as we know, the only house of an original immigrant that can be accurately located. Notice the north wall of the building; while it has all been plastered over you will observe that a portion of it, about ten feet high and extending back, is of a different shade from the remainder of the wall. It is thought that this is the old wall of Thones Kunder's original dwelling, and it is said, in the many plasterings the house has had, they have never been able to get the old portion and the new to be exactly the same shade.

The first meetings of the Society of Friends in Germantown were held at this house, and it was from the members of this little meeting that a public protest against slavery was issued as early as 1688. The paper was written by Pastorius, signed by him and three others, and, being appropriately referred to their monthly and quarterly meetings, it was forwarded to and weightily considered in the yearly meeting held at Burlington.

Thones Kunders was a dyer by trade. His death occured in the fall of 1729. He was the ancestor of the Conard and Conrad families. Among his descendants is included Sir Samuel Cunard, the founder of the Cunard Steamship Line.

One square west, on the south side of Manheim Street, at

HISTORIC GERMANTOWN

the southwest corner of Manheim and Portico Streets, is the house once owned by Jacques Marie Roset, born in France in 1765, who came to this country 1792. While passing up Chestnut Street on his arrival, with several of his countrymen, they met General Washington, who, recognizing them as Frenchmen, saluted them in French, "Bien vien en Amerique," an incident which Roset remembered with pleasure during his life. He died in his 80th year and is buried in the Lutheran ground. A daughter of his oldest son, Mr. John Roset, married the late Anthony J. Drexel. Notice the stone on the Spring Alley side of the house; also the one in front naming the street Manheim Square. Mr. Roset lived on the opposte side of the street. It was he who first introduced the tomato plant into Germantown.

Somewhat farther out, *No. 153 Manheim street*, is White Cottage, the home of the Betton family. Dr. Samuel Betton married a daughter of Colonel Thomas Forrest. Immediately opposite the house in Revolutionary times was Taggart's field, where the British infantry were hutted.

No. 5106 Main Street was occupied by Commodore James Barron in 1842, when in command of the Philadelphia Navy Yard. It was he who was in command of the Chesapeake when

HISTORIC GERMANTOWN

she was fired upon by the British ship Leopard, June 23rd, 1807, and who killed Stephen Decatur in a duel in the famous duelling ground at Bladensburg, Md., March 23, 1820.

The giant buttonwood tree, on the west side of Main street above Manheim, stood in front of what early in the last century was the Buttonwood Tavern, which succeeded "Ye Roebuck Inn," which was its name in Revolutionary times. There were two of these trees standing side by side. George Heft bought the property in 1819. The old inn was torn down to make way for the present house. The property is still in possession of the Heft family.

No. 5151 Main Street was the home of Philip R. Freas, who in 1830 started the *Village Telegraph*, later the *Germantown Telegraph*, for many years one of the most influential papers in the country adjacent to Philadelphia. When the Native American riots broke out in Philadelphia in 1844 the *Telegraph* was the only paper in Philadelphia which fearlessly upheld Sheriff Morton McMichael in his efforts to promptly subdue the riot. He edited the paper until 1885, when he retired. The little building next door was the newspaper office. In the rear of his home was a beautiful garden with rare trees and shrubbery, but this has now made way for rows of dwelling houses. Philip R. Freas died April 1st, 1886.

HISTORIC GERMANTOWN

No. 5140 Main Street was occupied by Gilbert Stuart, the famous painter, 1794-5. While living in Philadelphia his daughter says: "My father at this time was so inundated with visitors, he found it impossible to attend to his profession." He consequently removed to Germantown, occupying this house and fitting up a barn in the rear as his studio.

The second story or barn floor was used as the studio proper, while the lower floor was used to mix paints, etc. For many years, indeed until the barn was destroyed by an incendiary fire, marks of paint were observable on the walls. A small portion of the walls of the barn remained after the fire and these were carefully preserved and covered with ivy until within a year or two, when they were removed.

Here, on the authority of Gilbert Stuart's daughter, was painted the famous portrait of Washington, now in possession of the Athenæum of Boston.

The story is told that when Washington visited the studio for his sittings he was in the habit of walking into the garden and eating fruit from an apple tree which was standing within a few years.

On the authority of Watson here also was executed a full length portrait of Cornplanter the famous Indian chief.

Nos. 5203 and 5205 Main Street, formerly one dwelling

HISTORIC GERMANTOWN

house, is now well on to a century old. At one time it was occupied by Dr. Theodore Ashmead and later by Dr. Betton. Here July 14, 1860, was born Owen Wister, the distinguished story writer. His parents were Dr. Owen J. and Sarah Butler Wister, the latter a daughter of Pierce and Fanny Kemble Butler. The family were residing here temporarily while the house 5253 Main Street was being built by Dr. Wister. The Wisters continued living at 5253 Main Street until 1870, when they removed to Butler Place on the York Road. See reference to the latter in another chapter.

St. Stephen's Methodist Church was opened in 1856. The story is told that it was then such a plain and unpretentious building that it was often mistaken for a factory. When in 1857 a new pastor came to take charge, bringing his family with him, his daughter on catching sight of the building, exclaimed, "Oh! Papa, what factory is that?" "That, my daughter," he replied "is the factory I am going to work in." The present attractive building gives no indication of its plain beginning.

On this site stood the carpenter shop of Frederick Fraley. Tradition says that these shops were used for the manufacture of gun carriages for the American army and that they were burned by the British during the Revolution. Watson mentions that Washington was a frequent visitor at Fraley's carpenter shops. In later years the latter was a drum maker.

No. 5214 Main Street has been called the Hacker house, from the fact that for a long period it was occupied by Isaiah Hacker. It was at one time the home of David Hayfield Conyngham. It marks a position of the British Army's encampment in Germantown, as the following paragraph will disclose :

"The main body of the British occupied ground nearly at right angles with the main street. The front line on the Schoolhouse Lane to the west, and the Church Lane (its opposite) to the east. The park was in the area, south of the market-house, and fronting the house of David Deshler (now S. B. Morris'), in which General Howe had his quarters. The second line formed a parallel, at about one-fourth of a mile in the rear, and flanking the road near the old six-mile stone, before the door of H. Conyngham, Esq."—*Watson's Annals.*

No. 5219 Main Street was owned from 1775 until his death in 1795 by John Bringhurst. He was a prominent citizen of Germantown and one of the founders of the Academy. He was among the first to engage in the building of the well-known "Germantown" wagons. In 1780 he bu a "chariot" for General Washington, the price of which was £210 in

Price Homestead. Ladies' Club House, Manheim

HISTORIC GERMANTOWN

gold. Washington was particular that it have his "arms and crest properly disp'd of on the chariot." When Martha Washington set out for Mount Vernon in June, 1780, she rode in the new vehicle. Bringhurst's "Big House," southeast corner Main and Bringhurst Streets, now occupied by a store, is where Colonel Bird, one of the British officers wounded in the Battle, died, saying as he passed away: "Woman, pray for me. I leave a wife and four children in England."

In 1760 John Bringhurst and his brother George conveyed the ground used by the school to the trustees of the Germantown Academy. For many years John was one of the trustees.

The house *5253 Main Street* occupies the site of what was Christopher Sauer's home and printing establishment. Christopher Sauer, his wife and their son Christopher reached Germantown in 1724. Later they removed to Lancaster County, but father and son returned to Germantown in 1731. In 1738 he secured a printing outfit from Germany and in 1739 he began to issue the first German newspaper in America. In 1743 he issued the first Bible in an European language printed in America. This was forty years before an English Bible was printed in the colonies. Subsequent editions were issued by Christopher Sauer, 2d, in 1763 and 1776. Here also was printed in 1770 the first book in America on the subject of education.

HISTORIC GERMANTOWN

Christopher Sauer, the father, died September 25th, 1758. The son had become a Bishop of the Dunkard Church in 1753, but continued printing until the Revolution, when, because he would not take the oath of allegiance to the State, his printing effects were seized and sold. He died August 26th, 1784, poor.

The old house stood close to the street, with a building in the rear, where was the printing plant. The Sauers cast the first type made in America about the year 1772 or 1773.

"As Printing Types are now made to a considerable degree of perfection by an ingenious Artist in Germantown; it is recommended to the Printers to use such Types, in preference to any which may be hereafter imported.—*Pennsylvania Gazette, February 1, 1775.*

The house and outbuildings were removed and replaced by the present dwelling about the year 1860.

Nos. 5242 and 5244 Main Street, now a store, was formerly the Indian Queen, a noted tavern, which gave name to the street alongside. This was formerly Bowman's Lane, then Indian Queen Lane, and now Queen Street. It was about at this point the following incident occurred:

"The British, shortly after the Battle, concentrated in Philadelphia and vicinity. Directly after they left Germantown a troop of American horsemen came through the town upon their rear, so closely that a British surgeon, who had just left dressing the

HISTORIC GERMANTOWN

wounds of three American officers, prisoners in the widow Hess' house, was overtaken on foot in the street. When they were about to arrest him, W. Fryhoffer, who saw it, and knew the facts of the case, proclaimed his useful services, and he was told to walk to the city at his ease. In the meantime the three officers were taken as prizes and thus unexpectedly liberated. The same troop, advancing a little further, encountered a Quaker-looking man in a chaise, who, in trepidation, made a short turn at Bowman's Lane and upset, and thus exposed a large basket-full of plate. He and his treasure were captured and ordered off to headquarters."—*Watson's Annals.*

The Wister house, *No. 5261 Main Street,* was erected by John Wister in 1744, and the property is now in possession of his great grandson, Mr. Charles J. Wister. The stones for the building were quarried from a hill in the rear of the property and the joists hewn from oaks in the Wister woods, a portion of which is still standing. It was so much larger than the average house of the time that it was known as Wister's "big" house.

During the fall of 1777 the house had been left in charge of a German servant, Justina. The family had gone to Penllyn, Montgomery County, to escape possible annoyance by the British army, and it was while here that Sally Wister, a daughter of the house, wrote the ever charming Diary* giving

---

* Sally Wister's Journal will be found in Pennsylvania Magazine, Vols. IX and X; also in Howard M. Jenkins' Historical Collections Relating to Gwynedd.

HISTORIC GERMANTOWN

vivid accounts of country life at that trying and exciting time.

When the British entered Germantown the house was occupied by General James Agnew. On the morning of the Battle Justina was at work in the garden and as General Agnew rode away he advised her to seek a place of safety. Justina, however, worked away unmindful of the happenings around her, and it was not long before General Agnew was carried back to the house "bleeding at every vein." He was laid on the floor in the northwest parlor. His blood still stains the floor boards, having resisted a century and more of spring and fall cleanings. General Agnew was buried with Colonel Bird in the Lower Burial Ground.

No. 5267 Main Street, while one of the oldest-looking houses along the Main Street, seems not to possess any particular historical interest. Seventy-five years ago one Anthony Gilbert, a blacksmith who lived here, was noted for his great physical strength. He was known to write his name on a board fence with a piece of chalk with five fifty-six-pound weights hanging on his arm.

The house *No. 5300 Main Street*, now the parsonage of the Trinity Lutheran Church, was one of the Sauer properties. (See mention of the Sauers.) The Sauers were accused of

HISTORIC GERMANTOWN

aiding the enemy, and Christopher Sauer, the elder, suffered many indignities at the hands of the American soldiers.

There is a tradition that the type which was cast by the Sauers, the first to be cast in America in 1772-1773, was made in the cellar of this building.

Nos. 5275 and 5277 Main Street was occupied by the Germantown National Bank from 1825 to 1868. The Annalist, Watson, who was the cashier, is authority for the statement that this building had been at one time occupied by Thomas Jefferson, Secretary of State, and Edmund Randolph, Attorney General of the United States.

The yellow fever prevailing in Philadelphia, and Congress being soon to meet, Jefferson proceeded to Germantown, arriving there in company with President Washington, November 1st, 1793. The next day he wrote to his friend, James Madison:

"According to present appearances this place cannot lodge a single person more. As a great favor I got a bed in the corner of the public room of a tavern; and must continue till some of the Philadelphians make a vacancy by removing into the city. Then we must give him from 4 to 6 or 8 dollars a week for cuddies without a bed, and sometimes without a chair or table. There is not a single lodging house in the place (vacant?)."

HISTORIC GERMANTOWN

Jefferson no doubt was successful in finding a lodging in this house, for on November 17th he again wrote to Madison :

"I have got good lodging for Monroe and yourself; that is to say, a good room with a fire place and two beds, in a pleasant and convenient position, with a quiet family. They will breakfast you, but you must mess in a tavern ; there is a good one across the street. This is the way all must do, and all I think will not be able to get even half beds."

About the first of December danger from the fever having abated Washington and the members of his cabinet moved into Philadelphia.

East Penn Street used to be called Shoemaker's Lane for Shoemaker's big house which stood on the northeast corner of this and the Main Street. A short distance beyond the Reading Railway on the left hand side going out is the Rock House. Its origin is unknown, but it is said to be one of the oldest houses in Philadelphia. The low ground behind it at one time was called Mehl's meadow, and, with the Wingohocking Creek winding through it, it was a delightful spot. William Penn is said to have preached at one time from this elevation to the people assembled below him in the meadow. In this meadow before the Battle some of the British cavalry had their encampment.

Germantown Academy

HISTORIC GERMANTOWN

St. Luke's Church, at northeast corner of Main and Coulter Streets, was the first Episcopal congregation organized in Germantown (1811). The church then contained about twelve families in and about Germantown. The first building on the present site was erected in 1818 and it has been enlarged and altered many times since.

The Friends' Meeting (connected with Arch Street Yearly Meeting), occupies the grounds in the rear of the Linden hotel, northwest corner of Coulter and Main Streets.

It has never been fully determined just how many of the first settlers of Germantown were members of the Society of Friends, but a meeting was established very soon after their arrival. It first met at the home of Thones Kunders, now 5109 Main Street, and at other private houses. Jacob Shoemaker early gave the meeting three square perches of land, and the presumption is a log meeting house was erected on it. In 1693 he conveyed to the meeting fifty acres, of which the three square perches was a portion, and on this lot in the present old graveyard, along the Main Street, a stone meeting house was erected in 1705. This was replaced in 1812 by another building, which stood where the present school building stands, and this in turn was succeeded by the present building. The old stone has been placed in an adjoining committee building.

HISTORIC GERMANTOWN

"*Philadelphia,* June 5. Yesterday forenoon in the Meeting House of the People called *Quakers* at *Germantown,* died suddenly of an Apopletic Fit, *Isaac Norris* of *Fairhill,* Esq. ; who for a long time most worthily presided in the County Court of Quarter Sessions and Common Pleas, *Philadelphia,* was a Member of Council upwards of 30 years and been often chosen one of the People's Representations in the Legislature of this Province, as he was in this Year for the County of *Philadelphia.* His great Abilities in the Discharge of his Duty in each of these Stations, made him to be justly esteemed one of the most coniderable men in this Government."—*American Weekly Mercury, June 5th, 1735.*

In the Free Library, which is under the care of Friends of this meeting, will be found a photograph of the Protest against Slavery which has been referred to. (See 5109 Main Street).

The Masonic Hall, No. 5425 Main Street, occupies the site of a building in which at one time A. Bronson Alcott lived, and here the distinguished authoress, Louisa M. Alcott, was born. Mr. Alcott came to Germantown to take charge of a school. The following letter to Colonel May, dated Germantown, November 29th, 1832, gives the information in regard to the interesting event :

"Dear Sir:—It is with great pleasure that I announce to you the birth of a second daughter. She was born at half past 12 this morning, on my birthday (33) and is a very fine healthful child, and has a fine foundation for health and energy of character. Abba, inclines to have her called Louisa May, a name to her full of every association connected with amiable benevolence and exalted worth. I hope its present possessor may rise to equal attainment and deserve a place in the estimation of Society. Yours,

A. BRONSON ALCOTT."

The family removed from Germantown when Louisa Alcott was about two years of age.

No. 5430 Main Street was the home of Captain Albert Ashmead. His father, John Ashmead, lived next door above, 5434. When the British army entered Germantown, Thursday morning, September 25th, 1777, little John Ashmead, then a boy of twelve, sat on the front stoop and saw them pass—tired and covered with dust. While the Battle was in progress he ran out into the street, but was captured and taken to the cellar of 'Squire Ferree's home, nearly opposite. After the Battle he sallied forth and recovered two cannon balls, one an English and the other American, which have remained in possession of the family since.

Captain Albert Ashmead commanded a troop of country cavalry and escorted General Lafayette from Trenton to Philadelphia, when the latter visited this country.

William Ashmead, grandfather of Albert, was the first, soon

HISTORIC GERMANTOWN

after the Revolution, to manufacture the well known Germantown wagons, his shop being in the rear of these houses, and the house, No. 5430, was used as a show room, the ceilings being made high particularly for this purpose. When Captain Albert Ashmead married, the house was altered to accommodate him.

"The first introduction of carriage building was somewhat curious. Mr. William Ashmead, a smith, observing the heavy build of the coaches of his day, and that they were mostly imported, if intended to be of a superior kind, bethought him to form an open-front light carriage, on his own plan. When it was done, it was admired by many, and was often called for by the wealthy who wished to travel to distances;—among these was Mr. Bingham. They engaged it at a dollar a day, and it was in constant demand. At last, a gentleman from Maryland, who had seen it, came to the place to buy it. It was not for sale; but he offered £120 for it, and took it. Then another and another was built, and orders were renewed upon Mr. Ashmead. Soon, increased demand occurred; and his son John being made a carriage maker, received numerous orders for many kinds of light carriages, and especially for phætons. About the same time (the time of the Revolution and afterwards), Mr. Bringhurst, who was at the time a chaise maker, went largely into the making of carriages. Coaches and chariots were made for £200 and phætons for £100.

"The same William Ashmead, as a smith, had made himself a plough with a wrought iron mould-board, which was found to be a great improvement; and so much admired by Laf-

HISTORIC GERMANTOWN

ayette, who saw its utility, that he purchased four of them for his La Grange farm in France. No patent was taken; and in time some other person, following the hint, made the same thing of cast iron—such as is now in general use."—*Watson's Annals*.

The Market Square, now occupied as an open park, was the centre of the activity of the town. There was originally an acre of ground reserved from the Frankfort Company's land, but it was not centrally located, and was subsequently sold, and at the same time, in 1703-4, the Bailiff's, etc., "For the common good and to purchase a place nearer the now midst in the centre of said town," bought of James De La Plaine, a half acre representing the present Market Square. Here for many years and until recent times, was the market house. Here also was the engine house of the Fellowship Fire Engine Company, one of the three early volunteer companies of the town. For a complete account of this fire company see "Pennsylvania Magazine of History," Vol. xviii, page 429. The fire company removed to Armat Street in 1850 and the little old engine house was removed to the rear of 164 School House Lane, were it still serves as a play house.

Here also at one time was the prison, the stocks and the public scales. Delegations of Indians on their way to the city would stop in Germantown and were fed at the Market Square.

HISTORIC GERMANTOWN

A table often used for their dinner is still preserved by the Ashmeads.

Here, February 6th, 1764, several hundred Paxtang boys from the banks of the Conestoga and Susquehanna, then the frontier, on their way to murder the peaceful Moravian Indians who had taken shelter in Philadelphia, were met by Benjamin Franklin, Benjamin Chew, Thomas Willing, Thomas Galloway and others and persuaded to return to their homes. Philadelphia had been thrown into a state of great excitement which must in a measure have been communicated to Germantown, for the Lutheran pastor in the city came out to Germantown to warn his people not to take part with the mob.

The monument now occupying the square was erected in 1883 by Germantown to her soldiers in the Civil War. The principal part of the monument is built of Quincy granite. The top block, on which the soldier stands, is a piece of granite from Devil's Den, Gettysburg. The soldier is cut from Westerly granite. The four mortars were used for coast defence during the Civil War. The two bronze cannon on wheels were taken from the United States arsenal by Southern sympathizers during the war but were subsequently recovered by Union troops. One of them has cut upon it a Confederate flag and the name of a Confederate officer who was killed while serving the gun. The enclosure is made of musket barrels and bayonets used during the war.

Carlton

HISTORIC GERMANTOWN

The broken cannon on the north side was part of the armament of the British frigate Augusta, sunk by the American batteries while the vessel was attempting to reach Philadelphia during the Revolutionary War. The crown and British monogram " G. R." are on it. The muzzle was blown away by an American cannon ball. Some thirty years ago in removing obstructions from the river channel the vessel was raised and this gun recovered.

The shell on the south side was presented to the Confederacy by some friends in England in connection with a battery of Whitworth guns.

The cannon on the east of the monument has been in Germantown for many years and was used to fire salutes, etc.

On the sides of the monument are found :

Coat of Arms of the United States, with a quotation from one of Webster's speeches.

Coat of Arms of Pennsylvania, with a quotation from William Penn's writings.

Coat of Arms of the City of Philadelphia, with a quotation from the Gospel by Luke.

A badge of the Grand Army of the Republic.

The Memorial Tablets at the corners contain the names of Soldiers and Sailors serving for the Suppression of the Rebellion, and residents at the time of their enlistment in the 22d and 42d

HISTORIC GERMANTOWN

Wards, or who subsequent to this war moved into this territory and died there.

Tablet 1 contains, in chronological and alphabetical order, the names of those who died or were killed during the years 1861-65.

Tablet 2 contains, in alphabetical order, the names of those who died after 1865 and before May 30, 1900.

Tablet 3 the same, with the latter half of the alphabet, and

Tablet 4 the names of those who died between May 30, 1900, and January 1, 1901.

No. 5442 Main Street, the Morris house, opposite the square, was the residence of Washington during a portion of 1793 and 1794. It was built in 1772-3 by David Deshler. "As honest as David Deshler" is remembered of him. After the Battle Sir William Howe, who before the event had made his headquarters at Stenton, occupied this house. The house was later bought by Colonel Isaac Franks and by him leased to Washington who occupied it during the month of November, 1793, when the yellow fever drove many of the inhabitants of the city to safe places. An item in Colonel Frank's cash account is of interest : "Cash paid for cleaning my house and putting it in the same condition the President received it in, $2.50." The total payment, including the rent,

HISTORIC GERMANTOWN

was $131.56, which covered Colonel Frank's traveling expenses to and from Bethlehem, the hire of furniture and bedding for his own family, the loss of one flat iron, valued at one shilling, of one large fork, four plates, three ducks, four fowls, one bushel of potatoes and one hundred of hay."

In the following year, 1794, Washington occupied it during the heated period of the summer from July 30th to September 20th. Under date of September 24, 1794, the following entry occurs in his cash book: "Isaac Franks in Full for House rent &c. at Germantown pr rect, $201.60."

The house is about forty feet square, and it is said the front would have been wider had David Deshler not wanted to spare a plum tree which stood at the side. The yard at the side and rear has been kept in the simple elegance of the colonial time and is altogether a charming spot.

"General Washington while residing here in 1793 was a frequent walker abroad up the Main Street, and daily rode out on horseback, or in his phaeton. So that everybody here was familiar with the personal appearance of that eminent man. When he and his family attended the English preaching, in the Dutch Church, at the market house, they always occupied the seat fronting the pulpit. It was also his own practice to attend the German preaching, thus showing he had some knowledge of that language. His home was closed on the Sabbath, until the

HISTORIC GERMANTOWN

bell tolled, when it was opened just as he was seen coming to the church. . . .

"Many remember his very civil and courteous demeanor to all classes in the town, as he occasionally had intercourse with them. He had been seen several times at Henry Fraley's carpenter shop, and at Bringhurst's blacksmith shop, talking freely and cordially with both. They had both been in some of his campaigns. His lady endeared herself to many by her uniform gentleness and kindness. Neither of them showed pride or austerity. I could illustrate the assertion by several remembered incidents in proof."—*Watson's Annals*.

No. 5448 Main Street was built about 1760 by John Bringhurst, who has been mentioned (p. 46). It later passed into possession of the Ashmead family.

No. 5450 Main Street, built about 1790, was for a time the residence of Thomas Armat. It is said of him that during the war of 1812, when calling upon tenants for rent, if they were unable to pay, he would not only forgo his claim but aid them besides. He presented the town with hay scales in the square opposite, the revenue from which was turned over to certain beneficial societies. He kept a room in the house known as the "Ministers" room. He gave the land and was instrumental in founding St. Luke's Episcopal Church.

HISTORIC GERMANTOWN

Nos. 5452 and 5454 are also Ashmead houses. When they were built is not definitely known, but it is thought No. 5452 was erected about 1711, by John Ashmead, who came to Germantown from Cheltenham township in that year, purchasing a tract of 500 acres, of which a portion still remains in the family. The front of the house was rebuilt in 1790.

In March, 1742, Count Zinzendorf occupied No. 5454 and on the 14th of May he opened a school for young women with twenty-five girls and teachers. In June of the same year it was transfered to Bethlehem, where it still is in existence as the Moravian Seminary.

Like many of the properties along the Main Street, the land for these extended back a considerable distance from the Main Street.

"A large body of Hessians were hutted in Ashmead's field, out the school lane, near the woods; their huts were constructed of the rails from fences, set up at an angle of 45°, resting on a crossbeam centre; over these were laid straw, and above the straw grass sod—they were close and warm. Those for the officers had wicker doors, with a glass light, and interwoven with plaited straw; they had also chimneys made of grass sod. They no doubt had prepared so to pass the winter, but the battle broke up their plans. One of the Hessians afterwards became Washington's coachman."—*Watson's Annals*.

There is a story in the Ashmead family that during the

HISTORIC GERMANTOWN

occupation of the town by the British a young British officer was attracted by little "Polly" Ashmead and frequently visited the house. One day he stood before an open fire warming his back when the tail of his coat caught fire. Polly saw it but as he was a British officer she said nothing. When he discovered his coat was burning, and at the same time saw that Polly was laughing, he shook his finger at her, upbraided her for not telling him and called her a "little rebel."

From this family are descended, through Sophia Ashmead, who married, in 1843, Ellis Bartlett, an American merchant, the late Sir Ellis Ashmead Bartlett, a member of the English Parliament, and his brother, William Lehman Ashmead Bartlett, the husband of the Baroness Burdett-Coutts. They were both born in America but were educated in England and became British subjects.

William Penn once preached in the house of Jacob Tellner, which stood where the Savings Fund Building now stands, on the southwest corner of School Lane and Main Street. Dr. George Bensell pulled this house down to erect a handsome residence about 1795. This stood until 1880, when it was torn down to make way for the present building. The old doorway which stood in the Bensell house was removed through the efforts of Dr. William R. Dunton and placed in the house southeast cor-

Morris House

HISTORIC GERMANTOWN

ner of Main Street and Walnut Lane. There is a tradition that Jacob Tellner's house was the first stone house built in Germantown, and that William Penn was present at the raising of the roof.

The Woman's Christian Association building, fronting on the square, corner of Mill Street, was at one time occupied by one of the banks from Philadelphia, when the latter was driven out of Philadelphia by the yellow fever epidemic. Massive vaults had been constructed in the cellar to which the money was conveyed. This house was used for five years by the Episcopalians as a place of worship until the erection of St. Luke's Church.

Market Square Presbyterian Church is the third church building erected on this site. Originally built by the German Reformed Church in 1733, it was enlarged in 1762 and a steeple added. This building made way for a larger structure in 1839, which in turn was replaced by the present structure. Its first bell, cast in 1725, is still preserved in the church. Its weather vane, made of metal, represented a crowing cock. When the Paxtang were encamped in the square they amused themselves firing at the weathercock on the church. It still bears the marks of these bullets. It was removed when the present building was erected and is carefully preserved by Mr.

HISTORIC GERMANTOWN

Charles J. Wister. Count Zinzendorf preached his first sermon on landing in America here, December 31st 1741, and on June 17th, 1742, his last on leaving. At the time of the Battle a battalion of Virginians was captured and confined in the church building by the British until they were marched into the city. Here their tall figures, their wounds and powder-stained faces attracted much attention from the townspeople.

"The Ninth Regiment was in the hottest of the fight, and nearly one-half the whole regiment was killed and wounded. It drove every portion of the British Army with which it came in contact before it, and I was told by one of the officers that in the excitement of the moment, supposing every part of the American Army had been as successful as themselves, they had no doubt of reaching Philadelphia, the headquarters of General Howe. When the retreat of the American army was ordered, the Ninth Regiment was so far in advance of the rest of the army, that before they could join the main body they were surrounded and made prisoners. When surrounded they had made more prisoners than the whole number of the regiment. On the morning after the Battle of Germantown the prisoners were marched to Philadelphia."—*Joyne's Account, Ninth Virginia Continental Line.*

President Washington attended here when living in the Morris house opposite.

The Mutual Fire Insurance Company, northeast corner

HISTORIC GERMANTOWN

School House Lane and Main Street, occupies the site of the old De La Plaine house. At the time of the Battle it was occupied by 'Squire Joseph Ferree, and a number of weeping women and children found refuge in the cellar while the fight was in progress.

The Pennsylvania Council of Safety in 1776 ordered that the supply of salt and saltpetre be removed to Germantown, and presumably stored in Squire Ferree's cellar, as he was in charge of it. On the 8th of July of that year it was "Resolved that Dr. Charles Bensell, Joseph Ferree and Leonard Stoneburner be appointed to collect all the leaden window weights, clock-weights and other lead in Germantown and its neighborhood," for which the liberal price of six pence per pound will be allowed.

When Whitfield visited Germantown he preached from a little balcony to a great crowd gathered in the Market Square below.

"On Friday last the Rev. *Mr. Whitefield* arrived here with his Friends from *New York*, where he preached eight Times ; . . . He has preach'd here twice every Day, since his arrival, in the Church to great Crowds, except Tuesday, when he Preach'd at *German Town* from a Balcony to about 5000 People."—*American Weekly Mercury, Nov. 22 to Nov. 29, 1739.*

Visitors should see the Shag Rag, the old hand engine be-

HISTORIC GERMANTOWN

longing to the Middle Ward Fire Company, which is now carefully preserved by the Insurance Company in their office. It was imported from England in 1764. Water was carried to it in leather buckets, of which each member kept two hanging in his hallway ready for instant service. Three or four men standing on each side of the engine and working the handles up and down industriously could throw a stream of half an inch in diameter a distance of fifty feet or more.

The Germantown Bank, northwest corner Main Street and School House Lane, was chartered in 1813, and began business in 1814. It was first located in a house next to the corner, 5504 Main Street, but in 1825 it removed to 5277 Main Street. In 1868 it returned to its present location and later bought and absorbed 5504, the building in which it first started.

The corner house was known as Bensell's house, having been erected early in the eighteenth century by Carl Benzelius. The house was occupied for several years, until about 1806, by the Germantown Library.

"The Members of the *Library Company of Germantown* are desired to meet on Monday, the 6th Day of May, at the House of Daniel Mackenet, to choose three Directors and a Treasurer, and to make their tenth annual payment."—*Penna. Gazette, April 25th, 1754.*

HISTORIC GERMANTOWN

It was later altered into a store.

In 1776 Lieutenant George Ball, of the British Navy, a prisoner of war, was sent to Germantown by the Council of Safety. A letter was sent at the same time to Dr. Charles Bensell, desiring him to "provide proper lodging for the Lieutenant."

For a brief period, during the yellow fever epidemic in Philadelphia, 1798, Elizabeth Drinker and her son boarded with the widow Bensell. Elizabeth Drinker writes in her well-known Journal, August 22d, 1798:

"Half of her house is taken by other persons, but we are entirely separated, ye doors between locked up. Aug. 23d. Two Frenchmen lodge in the room adjoining us, with a door which opens into our room, which is locked and ye old lady has ye key. They were jabbering last night, but I could not understand them. They are nearer than I like; I stopped the keyhole this morning with paper."

Watson is authority for the statement that Generals Washington, Knox and Greene slept in 5504, which was next to the corner. This building was occupied by the Bank of the United States during a portion of 1798. Elizabeth Drinker records, September 25th:

"Ye United States Bank removed ye contents thereof, from Philada. ye 22nd inst. to Germantown—to the house lately occupied by Rochardet as a Coffee house or Tavern next door to

HISTORIC GERMANTOWN

S. Rhoads, escorted by a body of Light-horse. It occasioned a great stir in that neighborhood, where there was great abundance of it before.''

One square west of the Main Street is the Germantown Academy (southwest corner School House Lane and Greene Street), founded January 1st, 1760. With the exception of a period during the Revolution, school has been held here continuously since. It was originally called the Germantown Union School house. The little buildings were constructed for the masters. The school started with 131 pupils—61 in the English and 70 in the German department.

The following is an extract from an advertisement of the school in the *Pennsylvania Gazette,* March 5th, 1761 :

"The School-House consists of 80 Feet in Front, and 40 Feet in Depth, two Stories in Height, with six commodious Rooms for the Use of the several Schools. To which are added as Wings, two convenient Dwelling-houses, with a lot of Ground to each, for the Residence of the Masters and their Boarders.

"The Advantages of the School, with respect to Situation, must, if duly considered, contribute not a little to its Promotion and Encouragement. The House is built on a fine airy Hill, a little removed from the Public or Main street. The Air is known, from long Experience, to be pure and healthy ; often recommended, by the best Physicians, to Invalids ; and indeed the Place, without Exaggeration, may be justly termed the

Market Square

HISTORIC GERMANTOWN

Montpelier of Pennsylvania. The Opportunities and Examples of Vice and Immorality, which ever prevail in large Cities, here will seldom present themselves, to decoy the youthful Mind from its natural Inclination of Virtue. Its Retirement, for want of Objects to divert the Attention will fix the Mind to Application and Study. Its small Distance from the City of Philadelphia will enable the Citizen, in some Measure, to superintend both the Health and Education of his Child."

After the Battle the building was used as a hospital for the wounded, and several British soldiers are buried in the yard at the rear. The school was chartered by the State in 1786 as the Public School at Germantown.

The bell in the belfry has a romantic history. It was brought to Philadelphia in 1774 in the tea ship Polly, which was not allowed to land by the indignant citizens of Philadelphia. The cargo, including the bell, was carried back to England, where it remained until the war was over, when it was again brought over and put in place. A part of the weather vane is a crown representing the royal insignia of England, which has never been disturbed. In the Academy's possession are the telescope used by Washington at the time of the Battle and other interesting relics. The house on School House Lane opposite the Academy was bought in 1810. The Gymnasium along Greene Street is a modern building. The public is admitted to the school.

HISTORIC GERMANTOWN

In 1793, when, on account of the yellow fever in Philadelphia, it seemed as if Congress would meet in Germantown, the the use of the Academy was tendered, November 6th, to Washington as a meeting place, but owing to the abatement of the disease Congress assembled in Philadelphia December 2d.

In 1798, when yellow fever again drove the citizens of Philadelphia to the suburbs and country, the Academy building was occupied by the Banks of North America and of Pennsylvania. Elizabeth Drinker, who was then in Germantown, writes in her Journal:

"September 4 (1798). The Bank of Pennsylvania was this afternoon removed from Philadelphia, where it has lately been robbed of a considerable amount, to the school house in this town, escorted by McPherson's Blues.

"September 5. Germantown is like a beehive—the people swarm. About two o'clock, four wagons loaded with the cash, &c., from the Bank of North America arrived here guarded by the Light-horse men. They are also deposited in the same school house where the contents of ye other was yesterday lodged. This draws great numbers to this place. Fifteen or twenty people are guarding ye Banks."

No. 5506 Main Street, now modernized with a Mansard roof, was occupied during one of the yellow fever visitations by the officers of the State government, Governor Mifflin and Alexander J. Dallas, Secretary of the Commonwealth, having their offices here. When the building next south was torn down to make way for the addition to the Germantown National Bank, a doorway was disclosed, indicating that there was a connection between the two buildings.

Built in the wall of the rear building of this house is the head of an Indian made of some dark stone. It may be seen from the alleyway just north of the next house. Its origin and history are unknown, although there is a tradition that it was unearthed when the foundations of the house were dug.

Nos. 5516-5518-5520 Main Street, in Revolutionary times, was the King of Prussia Tavern. Its sign, which is still preserved, is said to have shown King Frederick on horseback and to have been painted by Gilbert Stuart while he was a temporary resident of Germantown. It was later painted over. In the rear there formerly stood a large barn which was used as a slaughter house by the British at the time of the Battle. The first stage coach with an awning was run from the King of Prussia to the George Inn, Second and Arch Streets, three times a week. About 1834 its use as a tavern ceased. The doorway on the second floor, at the south end, which has been closed up, shows where at one time it had been connected with the next house below.

HISTORIC GERMANTOWN

"*Andrew Weckeser* begs leave to inform the Publick,
"That he has opened a House of entertainment in Germantown, at the Sign of the King-of-Prussia, near John Jones's, Esq : where all Gentlemen, Ladies, Travellers, &c. may depend on the best usage. Their favors will be gratefully acknowledged by their humble Servant.   *Andrew Weckeser.*"
—*Pennsylvania Gazette, Dec. 15th, 1757.*

Standing back from the street next above the King of Prussia is an old hipped roof building, occupied at one time by Christian Lehman, who came to America with his father in 1731 with a passport written with gold ink on parchment. Christian Lehman was an importer of tulip and hyacinth bulbs, and is said to have imported the first English walnuts brought to this country. One tree of this variety still stands on the place. In this connection the following advertisement appeared in the *Pennsylvania Gazette*, August 4th, 1763 :

"To be sold during the latter Part of this Summer only, an Assortment of English double Hyacinth Roots, of a variety of Colours, as well as sundry other Sorts of Flower Roots, of various Prices, by *Christian Lehman*, in Germantown.
"N. B. He also keeps constantly for Sale some of the best English Walnut Trees, as well as other Fruit and Flowering Trees, of a Size fit to plant out, etc., etc. etc."

The First Presbyterian Church, Chelton Avenue west of

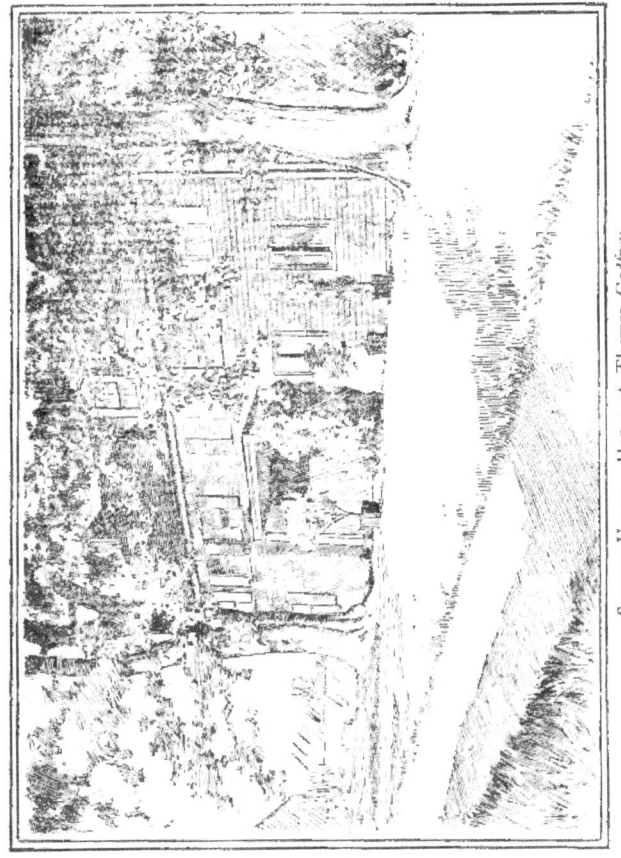

Spencer House. Home of Thomas Godfrey

HISTORIC GERMANTOWN

Main Street, stands where at one time was a famous orchard, and the steeple is directly over a spring. In digging the foundation it was necessary to drive piles on which the foundations were constructed. The orchard referred to was that of a German named Kurtz, whose house stood on the west of the Main Street where Chelton Avenue has been opened through. Kurtz was a great horticulturalist and botanist and his gardens contained many rare specimens. He was a friend of Matthias Kin, an eccentric man who was employed by German horticulturalists to collect seeds and plants for them. He spent most of the time exploring the wilds of North America, and it was to him that Kurtz was indebted for many of his specimens.

The First Presbyterian Church was formally located where is now the Young Mens' Christian Association Building, and the first meetings of the body were, before the erection of a church building, held in the Blair house, southeast corner of Main Street and Walnut Lane.

Vernon Park, on the West side of Main Street just above Chelten Avenue, now includes the old Wister mansion and some adjoining properties. Most of this land formerly belonged to Melchoir Meng, whose house stood along the main street immediately adjoining what is now No. 5708 Main Street. Melchoir Meng shared with his neighbor Kurtz a great love for

HISTORIC GERMANTOWN

trees and plants, and John Wister, who bought the property and lived here for many years, preserved and added to the collection. Some of these rare specimens are still standing, particularly noticeable being several great holly trees. Melchoir Meng was one of the founders of the Germantown Academy, and at the Battle his house was occupied by the wounded soldiers. His three daughters were alone in the house at the time, and the British officers assured them if they would go up stairs and stay there no harm would befall them. The house had been selected as a hospital on account of the numerous barrels of vinegar stored in the cellar, this being used to stanch the flow of blood. They saw the stricken Colonel Bird brought in and laid upon the porch, and soon the house was filled with wounded men.

Melchoir Meng's house was taken down when the city bought the property a few years ago.

Vernon Mansion was erected in 1803 by James Matthews, who, a few years later, sold it to John Wister, who lived here until his death. His son, John Wister, was a member of Congress and occupied Vernon until his death in 1883. The property now belongs to the city, and the mansion is occupied by the Germantown branch of the Free Library of Philadelphia.

No. 5845 Main Street was standing at the time of the Bat-

HISTORIC GERMANTOWN

tle. There is a tradition that at one time a mounted British soldier rode up to the door and demanded something. On being refused, he tried to urge his horse into the doorway, which was then guarded by a Dutch or double door.

The tollgate for the turnpike stood in the street just below this house and opposite Rittenhouse Street.

The Young Mens' Christian Association stands where for many years was the First Presbyterian Church. It was organized in 1809 as the "English Church" of Germantown. In 1811 the site was chosen, and in July, 1812, the building was dedicated. The church remained here until 1870, when it was removed to Chelten Avenue, the building after that date being occupied by the Young Men's Christian Association.

The First Methodist Church of Germantown was, until within a few years, located on East Haines' Street, a square or more east of the main street. The church was organized in 1796. There had been meetings of this body for some time previous to this date held, among other places, in the Academy Building.

The first meeting house was on the south side of East Haines Street (formerly Pickius Lane, later Methodist Lane, or Meeting House Lane) and was erected in 1804. In 1812 a large lot further out Haines Street was bought. On this lot a meeting house was built in 1823. The church building was later sold to the city and is now used as a public school.

On the south side of Haines Street, the first house east of Chew Street (about three-fourths of a mile east of Main Street), still stands a farm house that belonged to Christopher Ludwig. In 1777 he was appointed Baker General to the American army. He was an ardent patriot, possessed considerable influence, and is said to have been the original of Harvey Birch in Cooper's novel "The Spy." He was respected by Washington, and the latter, in 1785, gave him a certificate of good conduct, of which Christopher Ludwig was very proud and which he had framed and hung in his parlor. He was born in Germany in 1720. He had been a soldier in the Austrian and Prussian armies. He was a baker by trade and amassed a fortune in his business, an important part of which was making gingerbread. At his death he left much to charities. His grave is in St. Michael's Lutheran yard and consists of a granite topstone on granite pillars, with a long inscription giving an account of the principal events of his life. He died in 1801.

For further details see "Life of Christopher Ludwig," by Dr. Benjamin Rush.

The Town Hall during the war of the Rebellion was used as a hospital. Numerous frame wards were also constructed at

Green Tree Tavern

HISTORIC GERMANTOWN

the side and rear, so that eventually the hospital accommodated 630 beds. The hospital was organized July, 1862. It was called the Cuyler Hospital, in honor of John M. Cuyler, M.D., Medical Director, U. S. A.

The hospital was used until the end of the war.

The clock in the Town Hall was made by Lukens, of Montgomery County, and was formerly in the State House, Philadelphia. The Bell was the second one in the history of the State House, and is said to contain considerable silver to give it a "silvery" tone. The steeple was erected for it and the clock started in Germantown, October 4th, 1878.

No. 5938 Main Street is the Engle house, built by Benjamin Engle in 1758 and remains in the possession of this family to this day. The Engles were tanners in early days, and the tannery stood in the rear until modern times. The tradition is that Elizabeth Engle, standing in the doorway after the Battle, saw the wounded General Agnew carried by on a door. After the Battle the British soldiers were seen gathering up the American muskets and breaking them one by one over a cubical quartz stone which stood for many years at the gateway alongside the house to keep the wagon wheels from hitting the post. A good Engle horse was taken from the stable and a poor old English hack substituted.

HISTORIC GERMANTOWN

The house at the southeast corner of Main Street and High Street is known as the Morris-Littell house. Mrs. Ann Willing Morris lived here from 1812 until her death, in 1832. Of her two daughters who occupied the house, one was Margaret H. Morris, the first woman elected a member of the Academy of Natural Sciences. She was a noted naturalist, and it is said that to her belongs the credit of discovering the habits of the seventeen-year locusts, enabling her to predict their reappearance. It was on these grounds that the investigations were made.

This house, or a portion of it, was the home at one time of Dr. Christopher Witt, further mention of whom will be found in the succeeding paragraphs.

No. 25 High Street, just in the rear of the Methodist Church, was built about 1796 by Daniel Pastorius, a great grandson of Francis Daniel Pastorius. It then stood on the Main Street, next to the Morris-Littell house, with only a carriage drive separating them. When High Street was opened it was moved some fifty feet northward, and a few years ago it was moved once more to its present location.

Some thirty years ago Dr. Dunton tore down the old Pastorius house, which formerly stood between his house and No. 6019 Main Street, and used the stone in building the rear wing of this house.

Wyck

HISTORIC GERMANTOWN

Dr. Dunton has carved over his doorway the Latin motto, *Procul este profani,* which Whittier says was carved over Pastorius' door.

"Then through the vine-draped door whose legend read,
'Procul este profani!' Anna led
To where their child upon his little bed

"Looked up and smiled. 'Dear heart,' she said, 'if we
Must bearers of a heavy burden be,
Our boy, God willing, yet the day shall see

"'When from the gallery to the farthest seat
Slave and slave-owner shall no longer meet,
But all sit equal at the Master's feet.'"
—*From Whittier's Pennsylvania Pilgrim.*

In the rear, almost adjoining the church, is an old building, formerly a Pastorius farm house. The doorway, which is a particularly handsome one, was formerly in one of the Bensell houses on the Main Street above School Lane, torn down to make way for the Germantown National Bank.

St. Michael's Episcopal Church, on the south side of High Street, two squares east of the Main Street, occupies the site of the old Warner burying ground. Its walls may be traced by the stone foundation still showing through the sod. In addition to the graves of the two Doctor Warners, for whom substantial headstones are still standing, there are numerous other mounds without stones. Here is also buried, in a now unmarked grave, Dr. Christopher Witt (or Dewit, as it is sometimes spelled), who died in 1765, aged ninety years.

"Last week died at Germantown Dr. Christopher Dewit; a gentleman long and well known throughout this and the neighboring Provinces, for his great Services and Abilities in the Profession of a Physician."—*Pennsylvania Gazette, February 7, 1765.*

It is said that some of the dead from the Battle, English as well as Americans, are buried here, and for many years before the church was built the graveyard and the surrounding ground was called "Spook Hill."

No. 6019 Main Street was formerly the Green Tree Tavern. It was built in 1748. The letters "D. S. P" in the date stone stand for Daniel and Sarah Pastorius. The house was a public one kept by Daniel Pastorius until his death in 1754.

There is a well-founded tradition that during the Battle the attacking Americans, on the east side of the Main Street, under General Wayne, penetrated this far towards the centre of the town. It is referred to in the chronicles of the time as the "Widow Mackinnett's Tavern," and it was a famous resort for driving and sleighing parties from the city. Later it was called the "Hornets' Nest," from an immense hornets' nest that was

HISTORIC GERMANTOWN

kept here as a curiosity. The tavern was the resting place of many curiosities of the town and vicinity. In 1825, when Lafayette was invited to visit Germantown, the intention was to entertain him at dinner at this inn. The evening before the day he was expected it was concluded that the tavern would not accommodate the party, so a deputation visited the Chew House, where arrangements were made for the dinner, over which Miss Ann Chew, then a young lady of sixteen, presided.

Nos. 6021 and 6023 Main Street are Warner houses. The Warners were early identified with the Pietist hermits of the Wissahickon, and particularly with Dr. Christopher Witt, the survivor of this remarkable body. Watson is authority for the statement that Dr. Witt's interest in the Warners was first aroused by their giving him a hat to replace his, which had blown away. Be this as it may, the relations were very close between the old doctor and the family, and when the former died he left his big house to Christian Warner.

Dr. Witt was born in England in 1675 and came to Pennsylvania in 1704. He was one of the most remarkable men who lived in Germantown. He was a physician, botanist, scholar, musician, astronomer and lover of nature, originally one of the hermits of the Wissahickon, a friend of John Bartram, the botanist, and of other noted men.

HISTORIC GERMANTOWN

An oil portrait of Johannes Kelpius, the Hermit of the Wissahickon, painted by Dr. Christopher Witt, is believed to be the first oil portrait painted in America, 1705. It is in the possession of the Pennsylvania Historical Society.

"Dr. Witt was a skilled botanist, and upon his removal to Germantown, after the death of Kelpius, he started a large garden for his own study and amusement, and to him probably is due the honor of starting the first botanical garden in America. This was about twenty years prior to Bartram's purchase on the Schuylkill for a like purpose."—*The German Pietists of Pennsylvania, p. 406.*

It was no doubt through Dr. Witt's influence that two of the Warners, father and son, became physicians. The latter died during the yellow fever epidemic of 1793. Their graves are referred to in a preceding paragraph.

A portion of "Wyck," southwest corner of Walnut Lane and Main Street, is thought to be the oldest house still standing in Germantown. The present building was originally two houses with a driveway between them. Its halls were used as a hospital and operating room after the Battle and blood stains still remain upon the floors. Reuben Haines, who inherited the property, was a prominent man of his day. He greatly aided in the building of the turnpike from Chestnut Hill

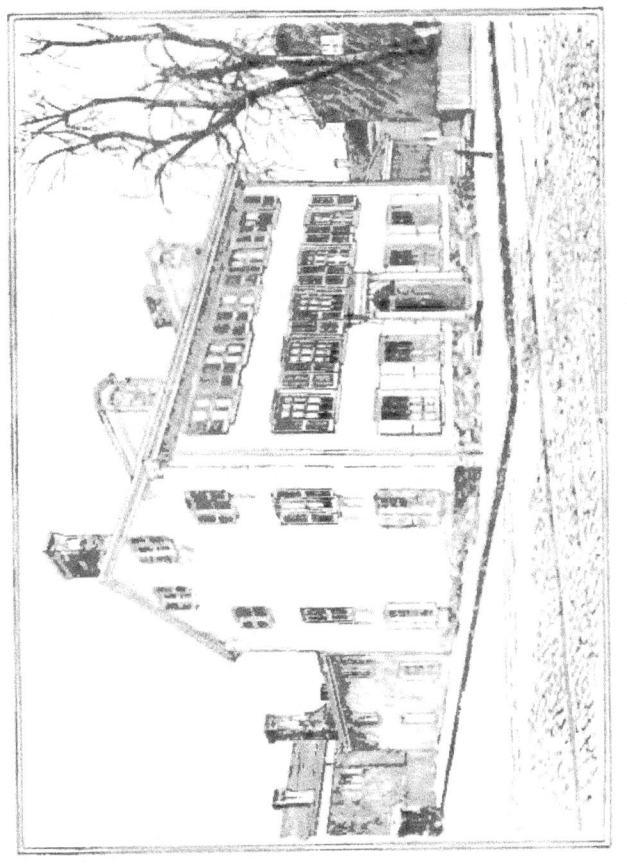

Blair House, now the Laurens

HISTORIC GERMANTOWN

to the city, and was active in other ways. When the Marquis of Lafayette visited Germantown, July 20th, 1825, he was entertained at "Wyck." Lafayette and his suite had previously visited the Chew House, then the Mount Airy College. On their return they stopped at "Wyck," where a reception was tendered him. He was addressed by Charles Pierce, Esq., and John F. Watson, the annalist, who presented him with a "box of great curiosity and value." During the reception Lafayette was seated in a chair that had belonged to Benjamin Franklin and which is still in possession of the family. The guests entered the front door and filed out at the back. From "Wyck" Lafayette went to the Academy and from there returned to the city.

Among the trees on the lawn of "Wyck" is a Spanish chestnut, a seedling from a tree General Washington planted for Judge Peters at Belmont.

In the rear of "Wyck" was the large old-fashioned barn erected in 1796 which, in 1890, was altered into a beautiful and comfortable dwelling standing on Walnut Lane.

No. 6043 Main Street, southeast corner Main Street and Walnut Lane, is a house of very considerable historic interest. The property was bought in 1775 by Dr. William Shippen as a summer home. Tradition has it that this was the first three-

HISTORIC GERMANTOWN

story house built in Germantown. It was the centre of a fierce skirmish during the Battle, and its plaster and woodwork for many years bore the marks of bullets, and the print in blood of a man's foot remained on one of the floors for some time. The house was also occupied by Dr. Shippen's son-in-law, the Reverend Samuel Blair, who was instrumental in establishing in Germantown the First Presbyterian Church. Services were at one time held in this house. Dr. Blair was elected President of Princeton College, but voluntarily made way for the famous Dr. Witherspoon. He was also a chaplain in the American army.

Later the Pennsylvania Manual Labor School was located here under the charge of Dr. George Junkin, afterward President of Washington and Lee University. One of his daughters married the famous Confederate General "Stonewall" Jackson. In 1832 Dr. Junkin removed to Easton to assume the duties of President of Lafayette College. The property in 1851 was owned by Charlotte Cushman, the famous actress. It was she who opened the East Walnut Lane, which she called Chestnut Street. The beautiful doorway was formerly that of a house which belonged to Dr. Bensell, at the corner of Main Street and School House Lane, now occupied by the Savings Fund.

HISTORIC GERMANTOWN

The house on the northeast corner of Main and East Walnut Lane was built in 1806 by the Rev. Samuel Blair, for his son, Samuel Blair, Jr.

The Mennonite Meeting House is on the Main Street, above Herman Street. As has been stated elsewhere, the little band o st settlers was composed of Friends and Mennonites. Here in 1708 the latter built a little log meeting house, the first to be erected in America, succeeded in 1770 by the present building. From behind a wall at this point a party of citizens fired upon the British troops as they marched up the Main Street during the Battle and mortally wounded Brigadier General Agnew, riding at the head.

William Rittenhouse, famous as being the first paper maker in the colonies, was the first pastor of the congregation.

No. 6205 Main Street was built in 1738 by Dirck Keyser, who came from Amsterdam with his son, Peter Dirck Keyser, in 1688. There is a tradition that this was the first two-story house erected in Germantown. Notice the initials "D. K. 1738," cut in the stones on the front of the house alongside of one of the windows.

Dirck Keyser was connected with the Mennonite Church. In Amsterdam he had been a silk merchant, and after he arrived

HISTORIC GERMANTOWN

here he wore a silk coat, which caused his neighbors some disgust. Some of the brethren calling to talk over his worldliness, found him in his garden. As he advanced to meet them he wiped his hands on his coat. They concluded, on seeing this, that he did not value it unduly and so said nothing of the object of their visit.

The Washington Tavern, *No. 6239 Main Street*, is an old building, and was known by this name as early as 1793. It is the type of a large number of taverns which in the early days lined the Main Street of Germantown. The Buck, Sadler's Arms, Green Tree, Indian King, Indian Queen, Crown and Cushion, Roebuck, Buttonwood, Fountain, Black Horse, White Horse, Lamb, White Lamb, Treaty Elm, and King of Prussia are some of the names of taverns that have now passed away. In the early times the capacious yard of the Washington Tavern could not accommodate all the teams putting up there for the night, and there would be an overflow row of wagons along the Main Street.

No. 6306 Main Sreet, the Johnson house, stood in the thickest of the fight at the time of the Battle. John Johnson, the occupant at this time, alarmed by the noise, went to his door to look out. A British officer riding by advised the family to seek

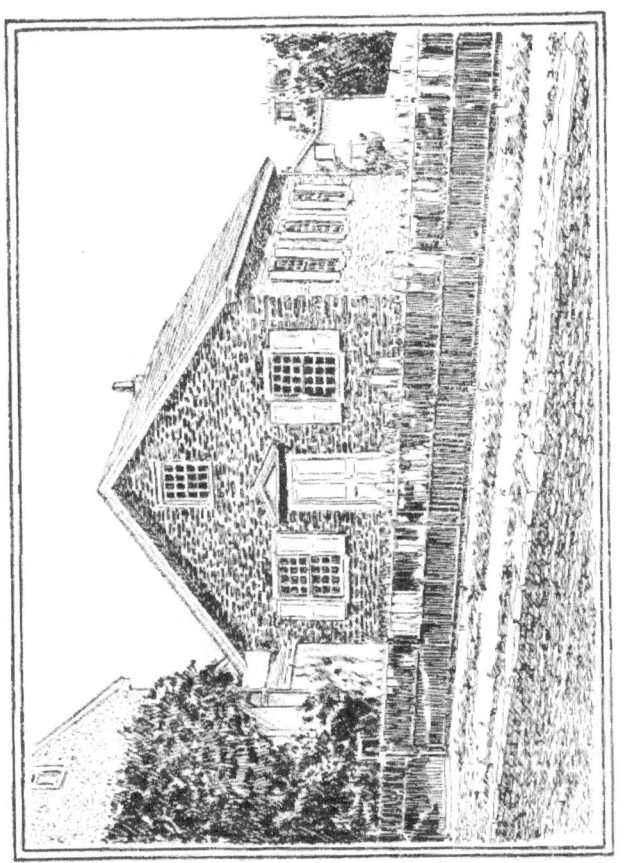

Mennonite Meeting House

HISTORIC GERMANTOWN

a place of safety. It was early in the morning and the maids had just brought in the morning's milk from the barn. They hastily left it and quickly sought refuge in the cellar. After the Battle the British soldiers swarmed through the house, drank the milk and cleared the kitchen of everything eatable.

A rifle ball passed through the house and the hole through the parlor door is still visible. A cannon ball knocked a chip out of the north corner of the house about two feet above the fence. The house is still in possession of the Johnson family.

The house was one of the largest and most substantial in Germantown when it was built, and on this account its building gave some concern to members of the Society of Friends, of which body the Johnsons were also members.

No. 6316 Main Street, now occupied by Mr. Ellwood Johnson, was formerly a Keyser property and back of it is still standing a cedar fence that was riddled with bullets at the Battle. The engagement back of this and the adjoining houses was particularly severe. The old fence, its bullet holes worn much larger by the winds and storms of a century and more, is now protected by another fence. During the engagement a bullet passed clear through the barn, striking an officer, who was carried to the rear of the tannery, where he died.

Separating this property from the Johnsons', adjoining, is a stone wall which was used as a breastwork, and this was one of the many obstacles that hampered the advance of the American army.

The Keysers were tanners and a portion of the tannery buildings still remains. There is also a millstone used for grinding bark which weighs nearly a ton, and which Nathan Keyser is said to have been able to lift at one time. Honey Run, a considerable little stream, used to flow across the garden in the rear.

No. 6307 Main Street was built in 1760 by Jacob Knorr. It stood in the thick of the fight at the Battle.

The fourth building above Washington Lane, on the east side adjoining the burying ground, is the Concord School House, built in 1775 for the upper residents of Germantown, who found the Academy on School Lane too far away. It was used as a school for many years and is at present occupied by the Charter Oak Library. Query: Why was it called Concord? Was it because the first German immigrants had come over in the ship Concord, or was it because its foundations were laid at the time when the shot that was heard around the world was being fired at Concord, Mass.?

The Upper Burying Ground of Germantown, sometimes called Ax's burying ground, from John Frederick Ax, who had

Johnson House, 6306 Main Street

charge of it from 1724 to 1756, is on the east side of Main Street, above the Concord School. Here are buried many of the early settlers of Germantown and their descendants. The oldest known grave is that of Cornelius Tyson, who died in 1716. Judge Pennypacker takes this to be the oldest existing tombstone to the memory of a Dutchman or German in Pennsylvania. Just inside the gateway are the graves of the Lippard family, ancestors of George Lippard, a writer of some considerable activity. In the east corner of the yard are the graves of several American soldiers killed at the Battle, including Lieutenant Colonel Henry Irwin, of a North Carolina regiment; Captain Turner, of North Carolina, and Adjutant Lucas. Over their neglected and almost unknown graves the annalist Watson erected a plain marble stone.

The little stone built into the wall at the right of the gateway gives the various dates when the wall was built and repaired.

For a detailed account, including a list of burials, see an article by Peter D. Keyser, in the "*Pennsylvania Magazine of History*," Vol. VIII, No. 4, and Vol. IX. No. 1.

The vacant lot adjoining the Upper Burial Ground is all that remains of Pomona, once a handsome estate extending along the Main Street to Duval Street and as far back as Morton Street. After the Revolution Pomona was the home of Colonel Thomas

HISTORIC GERMANTOWN

Forrest, an artillery officer from Germantown, later a member of the XVI and XVII Congresses.

The Ship House, *No. 6338 Main Street,* is so called from the plaster representation of a ship showing on its south gable. In early times it was a hotel with a sign showing William Penn's treaty with the Indians under the Shackamaxon Elm. The tradition is that the front part was built about 1760. In the rear was a large building, the first public hall in Germantown. The "Bulldog," one of the first three hand fire engines, was kept here. It is now in possession of the Bockius family.

No. 6347 Main Street was the residence for many years of Rev. John Rodney, who was the rector of St. Luke's Episcopal Church from 1825 to 1867, and rector emeritus until his death in 1886. The upper portion of the house was built by John Keyser and at the time of the Battle was occupied by him and his family. As the house was high up above the street, the family from their refuge in the cellar were able, by placing an apple under the outside cellar door, to witness the Battle in the opposite field. There is a tradition that a soldier officer fell near the cellar door and the Keysers, at his burial, saved the silver shoe buckles which he wore. Years after one of his descendants, searching for information as to his ancestor, was directed to the Keysers. It then developed that the officer they

HISTORIC GERMANTOWN

had helped bury was the person searched for and the buckles were given to the rightful owner.

The Chew House occupies the square bounded by the Main Street, Johnson and Morton Streets and Cliveden Avenue. It was the scene of the most important incident connected with the Battle. Indeed, the house and grounds have for a century and a quarter been pointed out as the Germantown Battle Ground. The place is called "Cliveden." The mansion was built about 1760 by Benjamin Chew, who at different times was Attorney-General of the Province, a member of the Provincial Council and later, Chief Justice.

Cliveden is two and one-half stories high and built of solid and heavy masonry. Back of it are two wings used for servants' quarters and kitchen and laundry; one wing is semi-detached and the other entirely so. Still further in the rear is the old stable, the whole forming a natural and admirable fortification, almost impregnable against any artillery which in that day could be brought against it. Along the front of the lawn there was, as there is to-day, a low terrace wall, and leading up to the house was a lane of good-sized cherry trees. Opposite was an open field stretching away to the banks of Paper Mill Run. The important part played by "Cliveden" in turning the fortunes of the day in the Battle of Germantown has been explained in another chapter.

HISTORIC GERMANTOWN

When Colonel Musgrave with his soldiers entered the house he ordered all the shutters on the first floor closed; a few men were placed at each window and the doors, with orders to bayonet anyone trying to enter. Most of the men then ascended to the second floor. He instructed them how to cover themselves and at the same time direct their fire out of the windows, adding that their only safety was in the defense of the house, that the situation was by no means a bad one, as there had been instances of only a few men defending a house against superior numbers; that he had no doubt of their being supported and delivered by their friends, but in any event they must sell themselves as dearly as possible. Some of the men climbed out of the back windows on to the roof and lying flat, fired over the front, and all disposed themselves to make a vigorous defense.

At the very first shot of the Continental cannon the front doors were burst open and some of the men were wounded with pieces of splintered stone. Captain Haines, a brave and intelligent officer commanding on the ground floor, ordered tables and chairs and everything available in the way of furniture, piled against the doors.

The Continental soldiers advanced under cover of the cherry trees in the lane and crouched behind the trees and marble statues as they fired at the windows above. One observer says the firing from the house was tremendous. The balls seemed to come

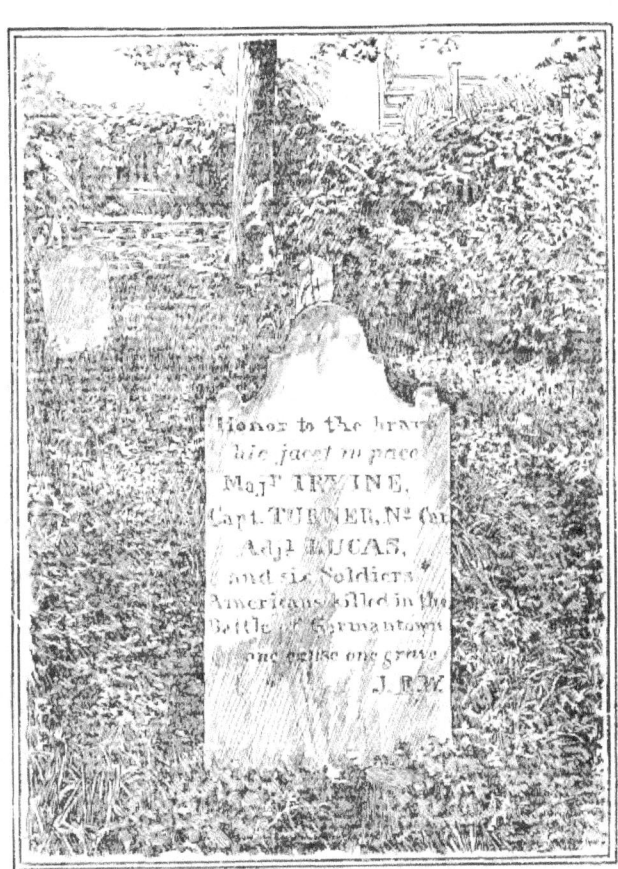

Grave Stone in Upper Burying Ground

HISTORIC GERMANTOWN

in showers. Several efforts were made to set fire to the house, and Major White, of Sullivan's staff, was killed in making the attempt. A bundle of straw was piled against the cellar window, but it failed to ignite the woodwork.

All efforts so bravely put forth by the Americans were unavailing. The house resisted every attack and Colonel Musgrave maintained his position until relieved by reinforcements. It is said the only man he had killed was in the northwest chamber on the second floor. No less than forty-six officers and men were killed in Maxwell's attacking brigade.

It was a sorry looking house that remained. The walls and ceilings were blackened with smoke and the floor stained with blood. In the front hall many holes are to be seen filled with plaster, plainly showing because not quite of the same color as the original. Not alone in the hall but everywhere, the plaster had been broken by cannon and rifle balls, the woodwork was splintered and the stonework shattered, the marble statues were knocked over, broken and disfigured. One six-pound cannon ball had entered the front window, passed through four partitions and had gone out at the back. Five carpenters, as well as other mechanics, were employed all the next winter putting it in order. The third story suffered more than the second, and the second more than the first. The ceiling of the second story was, and is, literally peppered with the bullets from the muskets

HISTORIC GERMANTOWN

of those who crept up as close as they could and fired into the second-story windows. Around the base of the column in the hall are still to be seen marks which are supposed to have been made by the butts of muskets stacked up around them.

The Chew family was away from home at the time of the Battle and the house but partly furnished had been left in the care of the gardener and probably other servants. There was among these a pretty dairy maid whom the gardener much admired. The dairy maid was rather pleased than otherwise when the red coats took possession of the house and was not inclined to resent their tender familiarities. Seeing this, the gardener remonstated with her, but without effect, and a "tiff" soon resulted. When the firing became heavy he urged her in vain to go to the cellar, and it was not until a cannon ball went through the house, making a great commotion, that the gardener, thinking further argument unnecessary, gave her a push which sent her headlong to the bottom of the stairs. He then turned the lock and left her in the cellar. Where he hid is not known, but they both came through the attack in safety.

The best position to view the house is from the gateway on Johnson Street. The house and grounds are not open to the public, but Mrs. Chew has not heretofore objected to amateur photographers and sightseers, who have a proper regard for the property, entering the grounds for a nearer view of the house.

HISTORIC GERMANTOWN

When Johnson Street was opened the graves of a number of soldiers were discovered who had been buried in the grounds. Miss Ann Chew had the remains removed, and they now rest under the clump of shrubbery close to the fence at the corner of Johnson and Morton Streets.

Upsala, on the west side of Main Street, almost opposite the Chew House, is thought to be one of the finest examples of the so-called "Colonial" architecture in this part of the country. The house was erected in 1798 by John Johnson, ancestor of the present occupants. It was three years in building. The cannon trained on the Chew Mansion, nearly opposite, were first placed where now is the front lawn of this house. For many years Upsala has been famous for its rare and beautiful trees.

The little old house at the northwest corner of Main and Upsal Streets was standing at the time of the Battle. It was for a long time the home of a certain Englishman, John Bardsley, a painter by trade, who some thirty years ago was sent to England through the influence of Germantown's then Councilman, William F. Smith, to bring over a lot of English sparrows to destroy the caterpillars, then infesting the trees of the city. It is believed that this was the first introduction of the sparrow on any great scale. The house has since been called Sparrow Jack's House.

HISTORIC GERMANTOWN

The Billmyer house stands at the northeast corner of Main and Upsal Streets. It was erected about 1727, and formerly was one house. At the time of the Battle it was owned and occupied by the widow Deshler and her family. It was at this house that Washington paused in his march down the Main Street at the time of the Battle, having discovered that the Chew mansion was occupied by the British. At that time there was no house between this and the Chew house. The tradition is that Washington stood on a horse block, telescope in hand, trying in vain to penetrate the smoke and fog and discover the force of the enemy entrenched in the Chew mansion. The stone cap of the horse block on which he stood is still preserved, and the telescope, is now in possession of the Germantown Academy.

The house later suffered greatly at the hands of the British soldiers who were quartered here. Its woodwork yet bears the marks of bullets and of attempts made by the soldiers to set it on fire. About 1788 it was bought by Michael Billmyer, a celebrated German printer, who here carried on his trade. The upper portion is still in possession of his family. Note the tablet erected by the Site and Relic Society.

The odd building adjoining the Meeting House, *No. 6611 Main Street*, was used as the parsonage, and parts of it are

David Rittenhouse's Birthplace

HISTORIC GERMANTOWN

said to be two hundred years old. Near it, in the Main Street, at the Battle of Germantown General Nash was mortally wounded and Major Witherspoon was killed by the same cannon ball. Major Witherspoon was buried in the yard adjoining. In later years his brother and sister came on from Princeton to secure his remains, but they were in such a condition that the attempts were abandoned and the body was again buried in the graveyard of the Lutheran Church, a short distance above.

The Church of the Brethern, or Dunkards, *6613 Main Street,* above Sharpnack Street, is the mother congregation of this sect in America. The Dunkards came to this country in 1719 and were gathered into a church organization in 1723 by Peter Becker, who was their first elder and pastor. They worshipped for many years in the homes of their members until about 1760, when they occupied a log building which stood in front of the meeting house. The front portion of the present building was erected in 1770 and the rear portion in 1897.

In the Meeting House a tablet has been erected to the memory of Christopher Sauer by Charles G. Sower, as follows:

HISTORIC GERMANTOWN

> In Memory of
> Christopher Sauer
> Bishop of
> Church of the Brethren.
> Born 1721   Died 1784
> Baptized 1737   Deacon 1747
> Minister 1748   Bishop 1753.
> Published the Holy Bible
> Second Edition 1763.   Third Edition 1776.
>
> ---
>
> Only son of
> Christopher Sauer
> Born 1693 in Laasphe, Germany
> Came to America in 1724.
> Commenced Publishing in Germantown 1738.
> Published First Am Quarto Edition of the Holy Bible
> 1743.
> Died in Germantown 1758.

In the graveyard are the graves of Alexander Mack, the founder of the Dunkard sect, who came to America in 1729, and of Harriet Livermore, the Pilgrim Stranger who is alluded to in Whittier's "Snow Bound," an eccentric religious enthusiast, the daughter of a Senator from New Hampshire. Her last days were spent in poverty in Philadelphia and as she was about to be buried in a pauper's grave a member of the Dunkard Church took her body and had it interred here.

At the Battle of Germantown this meeting house was a witness of the fighting. In the loft Christopher Sauer had stored some sheets of the third edition of the Sauer Bible. These were taken by the British cavalrymen who were encamped about and used as litter for their horses. Afterwards Sauer gathered as many as he could find together and had enough sheets to make complete Bibles for each of his children. Some of the paper is also said to have been used as wadding for the muskets of the combatants.

The old house *No. 6669 Main Street* belongs to the Lutheran Church, just above, and was used for many years as a home for the sexton. It is very old, but the date of its erection is not known.

St. Michael's Lutheran Church is at the *southeast corner of Main and Phil-ellena Streets*. It was founded about 1737. In 1742 the Rev. Henry Melchior Muhlenberg took charge of the two churches, one in Philadelphia and the other in Germantown. In 1746 the work of considerably enlarging the church was begun. Pews were placed in it in 1750. In 1752 a parsonage was bought. The present building is the third successive

HISTORIC GERMANTOWN

one that has occupied the site. At the Battle the parsonage was seized by the British and the organ was destroyed, the soldiers running along the streets blowing on the pipes.

In the graveyard are the remains of Christopher Ludwig, "Baker General" to the American army; also of Major Witherspoon, son of Rev. John Witherspoon, president of Princeton College, killed in the Battle, as well as those of many of the early settlers of the town.

At *No. 6749 Main Street*, George Hesser, at the time of the Battle, had just completed the cellar for his new house. Such a good-sized excavation proved too great a temptation for those who were burying the dead, and it was used for this purpose. Hesser was consequently obliged to abandon this site, and started again farther down the road. The old cellar is supposed to be about where the gateway enters on the north. The barn bears the date 1777, and was probably completed before the house. The property is now in possession of the Bayard family.

An account of life in Germantown, with some interesting local details during the yellow fever epidemic of 1793, will be found in Elizabeth Drinker's Journal. Henry Drinker, his wife Elizabeth, and a portion of their family, lodged with George Hesser from July 8th to November 16th of that year.

At *6843 Main Street* is the Paul house, occupied at the

Ship House

time of the Battle by the Gorgas family. The door jams contain bullet marks and there are other evidences and traces of damage. To save their cows the family penned them up in the kitchen. In the front yard, nearly opposite the window, at the left of the front door, stood a big linden tree in which four cannon balls found lodgment. During the century after the Battle, the heart having rotted away, allowed the balls to fall to the ground inside the hollow trunk. One morning Miss Paul was digging away at the root of the stump to plant some flowers, when out rolled the balls.

Back in a field in the angle formed by the Reading Railroad and Gorgas Lane and about equidistant from each, is the old Unruh homestead. The house is still roofed with earthen tiles under the later covering of tin. After the Battle wounded soldiers were quartered here. It is not known when the old house was built. The Unruhs came from Germany.

On the opposite side of the railroad is another old homestead, with a pond near the house and barn. The tradition is that the retreating soldiers threw their muskets into the water to save them from being captured. The farm is now occupied by a Mr. Wentz.

Occupying the site of the Lutheran Theological Seminary, on the east side of the Main Street, at Allen's Lane, was Mount Airy, the summer residence of Chief Justice William Allen.

HISTORIC GERMANTOWN

Later the house was used as a boarding school. At the time of Lafayette's visit in 1825 it was conducted by Benjamin C. Constant. In 1826 a Colonel Rumford was associated with him, and the institution was called "The American Classical and Military Institute." Many well-known persons received their education here, including Generals Beauregard and Meade, and the latter's brother. The building was demolished about 1846.

Mount Airy is now the name applied to this section of the Twenty-second Ward.

The Gowen House, *southeast corner Main Street and Gowen Avenue,* came into the Gowen family through the maternal line. Joseph Miller was born at Mount Airy, January 26th, 1757. In 1792 he built the house in which he subsequently lived and died March 27th, 1825. In it his daughter was born, who married James Gowen. Their son, Franklin B. Gowen, was born here. It was the home of Franklin B. Gowen for some years, then of his brother, James E. Gowen, who lived here until his death.

Log house, *northeast corner Main Street and Mermaid Lane,* is said to have been built in 1743 by Christopher Yeakle, who continued to occupy it until nearly the time of the Revolution, when he sold it and removed to the top of Chestnut Hill. It is the last building of the kind remaining in Germantown.

HISTORIC GERMANTOWN

EXCURSION, EAST SIDE OF GERMANTOWN

(The distance covered by this excursion one way is a little over six miles.)

AFTER visiting Stenton (see page 33), return to the Main Street. Just above Wayne Junction, turn to the right out Stenton Avenue to East Logan Street (formerly Fisher's Lane). Then east along Fisher's Lane, and at the bottom of the hill where the road crosses what used to be the Wingohocking Creek, is a little whitewashed stone dwelling said to have been used for the storing of powder and arms during the Revolution and also for the manufacture of gunpowder.

The mills are the Wakefield Mills, established at an early date by William Logan Fisher. His father, Thomas Fisher, in 1771 married Sarah, daughter of William Logan and granddaughter of James Logan, of Stenton. To the left, a short distance beyond the mills, standing back on a knoll from Fisher's Lane, is "Wakefield," the home of Thomas and Sarah Fisher, built about 1795, still in the possession of their descendants.

After passing Wakefield the Old York Road is soon reached.

HISTORIC GERMANTOWN

Turning up this road, the Jewish Hospital is passed on the right. Just beyond the tollgate, on the left, with a high wall along the road and a double balconied house with many outbuildings, was the home of Pierce Butler, a member of the Constitutional Convention and a Senator from South Carolina, He bought the property in 1812. He died in Philadelphia in 1822.

Fanny Kemble, having married Pierce Butler, Jr., lived at this place from 1835 until the fall of 1840. Many incidents in connection with her home here and of the neighborhood will be found in her "Records of Later Life," from which the following is taken :—

"Butler Place—or as I then called it, 'The Farm,' preferring that homely, and far more appropriate, though less distinctive appellation, to the rather more pretentious title, which neither the extent of the property nor size and style of the house warranted—was not then our own, and we inhabited it by the kind allowance of an old relation to whom it belonged, in consequence of my decided preference for a country to a town residence. . . . Subsequently, I took great interest and pleasure in endeavoring to improve and beautify the ground round the house; I made flower-beds and laid out gravel-walks, and left an abiding mark of my sojourn there in a double row of two hundred trees, planted along the side of the place, bordered by the high-road; many of which, from my and my assistants' combined ignorance, died, or came to no good growth. But those that survived our unskillful operations still form a screen of

Hall of Chew House

shade to the grounds, and protect them in some measure from the dust and glare of the highway."

Just about this point a British outpost was stationed along the York Road.

Proceeding to Branchtown, on the *northeast corner of York Road and Mill Street*, is the De Benneville graveyard. The house on the north, just beyond, was built by Joseph Spencer in 1746, bought by Dr. De Benneville in 1758, and named by his son "Silver Pine Farm." The Branchtown Hotel, immediately opposite, was erected in 1790 by Joseph Spencer.

On the left side of the turnpike beyond Branchtown and at the bottom of the hill is the entrance to Mr. Charles Wharton's place. Just inside the gateway is a rough stone some eight or ten feet in height. Here are buried four American soldiers surprised and shot by the British as they met around their camp fire, 1777. For a further account of the York Road and places beyond this point, see "The Old York Road and its Associations," by Mrs. Anne De Benneville Mears, published in 1890.

Returning to Church Lane (Mill Street), which intersects the York Road at Branchtown, and proceeding west (towards Germantown), at the bottom of the hill, about half a mile from Branchtown, the road crosses what used to be Wingohocking Creek. Within a few years the road has been filled up and the

HISTORIC GERMANTOWN

creek is barely visible on the left of the road; in the northeast angle of the creek and the road was Roberts' Mill, built in 1683, the first in the county. It was built by Richard Townsend, one of the passengers in the Welcomer with William Penn. Later it was sold to the Lukens family and it will be found plotted on the Revolutionary maps as Lukens' Mill. Early in the century it passed to Hugh Roberts, and as Roberts' Mill it existed until about 1873.

"As soon as Germantown was laid out, I settled my tract of land, which was about a mile from thence, where I set up a barn and a corn mill, which was very useful to the country round. But there being few horses, people generally brought their corn upon their backs, many miles. I remember, one had a bull so gentle, that he used to bring the corn on his back."—*From the Testimony of Richard Townsend, 1727.*

On the rise of ground back of the mill the British had a small redoubt guarding their encampment in Germantown. Here is the Roberts mansion built early in the last century, now unoccupied and fast falling to decay.

Retracing our steps a short distance, at the northeast corner of Church Lane and Dunton Street, standing back from the road and fronting west, with a little white spring house in front on the meadow bank, is the old Spencer farm house, which had been the birthplace and home of Thomas Godfrey, the inventor

HISTORIC GERMANTOWN

of the quadrant. At his death in 1749 he was buried on the farm, but many years later his remains were removed to Laurel Hill Cemetery through the efforts of John F. Watson, the annalist. During the removal the bones were deposited in the mill just mentioned, and Hugh Roberts, then a boy, relates how he ran for his life on unexpectedly opening the mill door and discovering the grinning skull there in the dusk of the evening.

> "To guide the sailor in his wandering way,
> See Godfrey's toils reverse the beams of day,
> His lifted Quadrant to the eye displays
> From adverse skies the counteracting rays;
> And marks, as devious sails bewilder'd roll,
> Each nice gradation from the stedfast pole."
> —*From the Vision of Columbus, by Joel Barlow, 1787.*

When the yellow fever drove the officers of the government to Germantown some of them lodged here, and George and Martha Washington were at one time calling. Hepzibah Spencer, the daughter of the house, then a child of four, crept up and peeped in the parlor window to see Mrs. Washington. After taking a look she turned to her companion and remarked in deep disgust: "Why, she's nothing but a woman, after all."

Back of the house is the old brew house.

Returning to the Limekiln Pike, and turning up it about half a mile, we reach Pittville. Here, occupying the Bayard

HISTORIC GERMANTOWN

property, northwest corner of Haines Street and Limekiln Turnpike, is the Philadelphia National Cemetery with many rows of the dead of the War of the Rebellion.

The third house above the tollgate on the right, lately remodeled, is what was called in Revolutionary times the Andrews place, now the home of Mr. Middleton. The left wing of General Washington's army moved down this road and a sharp encounter occurred with an outpost of the British at this point. Isaac Woods, who was standing in a cellar door watching the fighting, was killed by a stray bullet.

Returning to Haines Street and continuing on it westward towards Germantown, the Township Line, anciently dividing Germantown from Bristol Township, is crossed in about a quarter of a mile. On the east side of Township Line, about a hundred yards north of Haines Street, high up on the bank above the road, is an old house that at one time was the home of Colonel Thomas Forrest, a resident of Germantown and an artillery officer in the Battle. Continuing on Haines Street, about one hundred yards beyond the Township Line, is the old Kulp family burial ground, the walls of which are fast falling to ruin. A quarter of a mile beyond, the first farm house on the left, standing close to the road, is a house that was the home of Christopher Ludwig, "Baker-General" to the American Army. Reference has already been made to this. (See p. 90.)

Hillyer House

HISTORIC GERMANTOWN

Almost opposite is "Awbry," the park-like grounds containing the houses of the Cope and Haines families.

A short distance beyond is Chew Street.

On the east side of Chew Street, some four squares north of Haines Street, standing back from the street, is the Griffith House, which witnessed severe fighting at the time of the Battle.

Continuing on to Gorgas Lane and turning east on it, the tourist will find down in a field alout three hundred yards south of Gorgas Lane and as many from the railroad, the little Unruh house. (See p. 131)

Having now reached this point, the sightseer, if still ambitious, may cross over to the west side of Germantown, up Chew Street to Mount Airy Avenue, to Main Street, to Allen's Lane, to Livezey's Lane, and take in reverse order the excursion described in the following chapter.

EXCURSION, WEST SIDE OF GERMANTOWN

(The distance covered by this excursion one way is about six miles.)

STARTING at the Wayne Avenue end of Wayne Junction, thence up Wayne to Apsley, to Pulaski, to West Logan, to Morris, to Clapier, to McKean Street. At the foot of McKean Street is Fern Hill, formerly the estate of Louis Clapier, a famous merchant in the China and India trade. In 1812 one of his ships, the Dorothea, was given up as lost at sea or captured by the English, but she came safely into port, bringing her owner a rich return. On purchasing this property in Germantown he placed an iron model of the Dorothea on the barn as a weather vane, where it still remains. The estate was sold to Henry P. McKean in 1842. His son, Thomas McKean, built a yacht which was named the Dorothea; this boat was purchased by the Government during the Spanish War. The story of the vane and its connection with the yacht being made known to Secretary of the Navy Long, he retained the name Dorothea.

Watson says: " In the year 1789, a Resolution passed the

HISTORIC GERMANTOWN

House of Representatives, then in session in New York, that the permanent seat of government ought to be on the banks of the Susquehanna, in Pennsylvania; but it was amended in the Senate by fixing upon Germantown as its site. Upon being returned to the House, the amendment was approved and sent back again to the Senate, for a slight amendment, providing that Pennsylvania laws should continue in force, in such Federal district, until Congress should legislate otherwise. Thereupon, the subject was postponed until the next session; and thus, our old Germantown, after being fixed upon by both Houses, was wholly laid aside!"

It is the understanding that the plateau and bluff which enjoys an extended outlook over the city and is now occupied by Fern Hill was one of the tracts of land intended for the location of the Capitol.

Proceeding northward on McKean Avenue two squares, the grounds of the Germantown Cricket Club are reached. The large old house at the right of the entrance is a Fraley house. In 1798 Henry Fraley and his son John purchased from Joseph Shippen a tract which they proceeded to develop by opening streets and laying out lots. They called it the village of Manheim. Federal, Columbia and Tammany Streets were among those named and laid out. Either the venture was not a success or the lots were bought by those who wished large

HISTORIC GERMANTOWN

tracts of land, for all traces of the proposed village long ago dissappeared.

The frame building a hundred feet within the entrance formerly stood close to Manheim Street and was the country seat of the Price family. It is now the Ladies' Club House. Visitors should note the bronze tablet the directors have placed on the building and on the old Price stable, now a club house used by the Junior members; they should also visit the old-fashioned garden with its sun dial and graveled walks. When Germantown was occupied by the British the level plain about here was covered with a portion of the encampment. They destroyed the fences, using them for firewood and for constructing shelters, which they roofed with straw and with sods to hold them in place.

Leaving Manheim and proceeding westward to Wissahickon Avenue, or Township Lane, for it divides Germantown from Roxborough, thence along Wissahickon Avenue two squares to Queen Lane, and westward out Queen Lane about two squares, we come to Carlton, a long white building with a beautiful setting of trees, on a knoll at the right. This was the mansion of Henry Hill, erected on the site, or perhaps including an old farm house which also belonged to him, and was Washington's headquarters on two occasions, the first week in August, 1777, and again for two days in September, before and immediately after the Battle of Brandywine.

HISTORIC GERMANTOWN

When the British army occupied Germantown the Hessian detachment occupied the left wing from the village to the Schuylkill and General Knyphausen had his headquarters here.

Some years ago the lawn, having become full of weeds, was plowed up, yielding a plentiful crop of English coins.

Continuing on past the house towards the Queen Lane reservoir, we come to a granite stone erected by the Sons of the Revolution in 1895 to commemorate the encampment of the American army at this point.

Proceeding one square north to Midvale Avenue, the street back of Carlton, there is a much closer view of the house and the barn. Built in the high stable wall is a stone with this inscription :—

This tablet was taken from an old farm house nearby which will soon have crumbled entirely away and placed in its present position by Mr. Smith, the owner of Carlton.

Returning to Wissahickon Avenue and turning northward five squares above, at the bottom of a steep hill we come to Rittenhouse Street; turn

> Ruined by
> the war
> 1777
> rebuilt
> more firmly
> by the
> trusty
> Isaac Tustin.

to the left and follow it down to Lincoln Drive. Almost directly opposite the junction of the streets is a little house,

HISTORIC GERMANTOWN

below the level of Lincoln Drive, that was the birthplace of David Rittenhouse, Pennsylvania's first and greatest astronomer. The house was erected in 1707, and David Rittenhouse was born here April 8th, 1732. Soon after his parents moved to near Norristown. David Rittenhouse, besides being a famous astronomer, was elected President of the Philosophical Society in 1791 and served until his death; Treasurer of the State from 1777 to 1789; Director of the Mint from 1792 to 1795. He died 1796.

William Rittenhouse, the first of the name in America, arrived in 1690, and was the first paper maker in the Colonies. The mill was located near this house. It was washed away by a freshet in 1701 and another built; this in time was succeeded by another, and it by a fourth in 1780. The little stream was Monoshone Creek, but the popular name is Paper Mill Run. William Rittenhouse was an early Mennonite preacher. His oldest son was Mathias Rittenhouse, whose youngest son was Nicholas Rittenhouse, and David Rittenhouse was the latter's oldest son.

Up to within a few years there was a cluster of houses around the roads at this point and the settlement was called Rittenhouse Town.

Returning along Lincoln Drive to Wissahickon Avenue, we cross Paper Mill Run over an old county bridge, and continu-

Parsonage of Dunkard Church

HISTORIC GERMANTOWN

ing northward past Blue Bell Hill, as the settlement on Wissahickon Avhnue at Walnut Lane is called, in about three-quarters of a mile a long white house on the west side of the road is reached, called "Spring Bank," for many years the summer home of the Hon. John Welsh. During his life Mr. Welsh donated several acres to the Park, including Molly Runker's Rock, almost in the rear of Spring Bank, where later he erected the heroic statue of William Penn, which overlooks the Valley of the Wissahickon. It is marked with the single expressive word "Toleration." Mr. Welsh died April 10th, 1886. The property is now in possession of his daughter, Mrs. Smith.

Two hundred yards further on Kitchen's Lane is reached. Turning down it at the bottom of the hill is the Wissahickon Valley and Creek. Here on the east bank of the stream, near the summit of a hill and about two hundred yards north of the road, is the "Monastery." It was erected by Joseph Gorgas between the years 1746-52 upon the site of a log cabin erected in 1737, which was used as a community house by German Dunkard enthusiasts and was called on this account the Kloster. This house, so far as known, was never used for any monastic purpose. Right at the foot of the house, along the banks of the stream, was the Baptistry where the Dunkards baptized their converts. The Monastery is now within the limits of the

HISTORIC GERMANTOWN

Park. It is a short distance from here down the Bridle Path to the statue of William Penn, referred to above.

Returning to Wissahickon Avenue and continuing northward after crossing another one of the old country bridges and climbing a hill, Allen's Lane is reached, Wissahickon Avenue ending in it. A few hundred feet east Livezey's Lane takes off from it still in a northerly direction. This, too, leads down to the Wissahickon at what was Livezey's Mill, a famous one in its time. The old Livezey house is still standing. During the Revolution Thomas Livezey hid several casks of wine by sinking them in his dam. Some of it was still preserved within recent years. At the time of the Battle Thomas Livezey, hearing the roar of the cannon, climbed the hill and climbed on a fence to get a view of the fighting, but a stray bullet broke a limb off the tree under which he was. He concluded it was best to return to the house. Descendants of the Livezeys, of the same name, still own considerable land in the vicinity.

Not far above the Livezey house, along a pleasant and easy path along the Wissahickon where Cresheim Creek flows into it, is the Devil's Pool.

From this point the tourist may either return by the Wissahickon Drive or by crossing over to Gorgas Lane on the east side of the Main Street, the excursion planned for the east side of Germantown may be taken reversely, bringing one eventually back to Wayne Junction.

BATTLE *of* GERMANTOWN

AFTER the defeat of the American Army at the Brandywine in the month of September, 1777, and the occupation of Philadelphia by the British Army, General Washington reinforced by detachments from the Northern army and by the Militia of New Jersey and Pennsylvania, took up a strong position twenty-five miles from the city near the Perkiomen, a creek emptying into the Schuylkill. The bulk of the British army was posted at Germantown with a view to command the approaches to the city and overawe the surrounding country. The Market Square was the centre of the line. The right extended along Mill street to Luken's (Roberts') mill and was composed of the Grenadier Guards and six battalions of the Line, the whole under General Grant. The left extended along School House Lane to Ridge Avenue, and was composed of the Third and Fourth Brigades under Generals Grey and Agnew, and the Hessians, who were on the extreme left with a picket at the Wissahickon, the whole under Lieutenant General Knyphausen. Two battalions of the guard were posted in the rear of the town near to Fisher's Lane. General Howe's

HISTORIC GERMANTOWN

headquarters were at Stenton, the house of Dr. George Logan, at that time in England. Two battalions were in advance of the centre on the Main Street, the Fortieth Regiment at the Chew house, and the other, the Fifty-second Light Infantry, at Mount Airy, with a picket at the place of Chief Justice Allen, afterwards James Gowen's property. A battalion was stationed in advance of the right on the Limekiln Turnpike at Washington Lane, and the Queen's Rangers, a provincial organization, were posted in the rear of the right on the York Road below Branchtown.

The American commander, having received information that a portion of the enemy's force had been detached to assist in the reduction of the forts on the Delaware, determined to strike a sudden blow upon the army posted at Germantown and secure, if possible, a victory. After due consultation it was proposed to march to a point on the Skippack Road, about eighteen miles from the British position in Germantown, arriving on the morning of the 3rd of October, and to give the impression of forming a permanent camp at that place. That night the whole army was ordered to move at seven o'clock down the Skippack Road to the Bethlehem Turnpike and there separate at certain points into four columns, each to move by a separate route. On the morning of the 3rd of October, 1777, the American army arrived at the proposed distance from the

HISTORIC GERMANTOWN

British line and went into camp with headquarters at the house of Mr. J. Wentz, and at 7 o'clock that evening again took up the line of march. At the White Marsh Church General Smallwood with the militia of Maryland and New Jersey moved into the York Road to get in the rear of the British right. General Green with his own division and that of General Stephens and the Brigade of General McDougall marched on to the Limekiln Road to attack the British right. The rest of the army marched on down the Bethlehem Turnpike to Chestnut Hill, near which General Armstrong with the Pennsylvania militia, guided by George Danenhower, a soldier and a native of Germantown, continued over to the Ridge Road, down which they marched to get in the rear of the British left. The remainder of the army, composed of Sullivan's and Wayne's divisions, with the brigade of General Conway, the whole under the command of General Sullivan, followed by the reserve division under Lord Stirling, accompanied by the Commander-in-Chief with his staff, marched by the main road down through Chestnut Hill to the village of Germantown to attack the enemy's left. You will thus see how extended was the plan of attack and will appreciate how necessary it was in order to achieve success that its different parts should work together without friction or failure.

The several days preceding October 4th had been fair and

HISTORIC GERMANTOWN

delightful but the mornings had been noticeably foggy. When General Sullivan's division reached the Mermaid Tavern at the northern boundry of Mount Airy, where Cresheim Creek crosses the Main Street, the sun was just rising above the hills, but it soon buried itself in a bank of cloud, and a fog more dense than usual settled over the town. Some chronicles have stated that at times it was difficult to see a hundred feet away, others have said a hundred yards. It is probable that the shifting fog clouds rolling in waves would now and then lift and give at times a wider range of vision, but soon the smoke of battle and of burning stubble fields, hay and other combustibles, added to the fog, made a darkness in which there was no discovering friend from foe. To prevent mistaking each other, the soldiers and officers had been ordered to place a piece of white paper in their hats, but this precaution if obeyed was ineffective; to make matters worse, Thomas Paine, who was present at the Battle, says that the Americans were rendered suspicious of each other by many of them being dressed in red.

General Sullivan's division formed on the right of the road, which would be the west, and General Wayne on the east. Sullivan was the first to come into action, attacking the picket at the Allen house and killing all the sentries, he carried all before him and drove the enemy in confusion until at last they, with reinforcements from below, were able to make a stand on

Old Doors at Chew House

HISTORIC GERMANTOWN

both sides of the Main Street at the Mennonite Church below Tulpohocken Street. To the east of the road General Greene also pushed on and passed the Chew House.

In the meantime Washington, with the reserve divisions, had arrived at the Billmyer House, about which time it was discovered that six companies of the 40th Regiment under command of Colonel Musgrave, during the retreat from Mount Airy, had taken refuge in the Chew House, and barricading the doors and windows of the first story were keeping up a steady fire from the upper windows upon the road and its vicinity. Both Sullivan's and Greene's divisions had passed the house before its occupancy by the British had been discovered. After a council of war held near the Billmyer House Washington ordered the attack upon the Chew House by Maxwell's Brigade of the reserve and sent the other brigade of the reserve, Nash's, to strengthen Sullivan's line at Washington Lane.

Meanwhile General Greene had commenced fighting on the Limekiln road, and after some delay, owing to the fog, in which the division of General Stephen's had gone astray and the brigade of McDougall had gone too far to the left, he formed his own division in line just above Pittville, and moving over the fields, made a vigorous attack upon the British right, capturing the redoubt near Lukens' mill and was in a fair way to penetrate into the town at Market Square.

HISTORIC GERMANTOWN

By this time also Armstrong, on the Ridge Road, had arrived in front of the Hessians and was skirmishing with them, using his field pieces on the heights above the Wissahickon.

The battle was now general along the line, except on the York Road, where Smallwood was approaching Branchtown. Sullivan, reinforced by Nash's brigade, began to push the enemy towards the centre of the town. It seemed at this time as if the British army was practically defeated; the utmost consternation prevailed and orders were actually given for the various corps to rendezvous at Chester. Unfortunately at this moment a panic arose in General Wayne's command by some one calling out that they were surrounded, and the continuons firing at the Chew house, together with the approach in the rear of one of General Greene's brigades, which had gone astray in the fog and was mistaken for the enemy, and the beating of a drum at the Chew house, supposed to be a signal for retreat, all combined to throw Wayne's division into confusion, and despite the remonstrances of their officers, the troops began to retreat.

The retirement of Wayne uncovered the left of Sullivan, and his line being somewhat extended and disordered and his ammunition exhausted, he was compelled to give the order to retire. Washington fearing a general rout, sent messengers to recall Smallwood and Armstrong, as well as Greene, who was still successfully engaged with the enemy and who was forced also to re-

HISTORIC GERMANTOWN

ceive an attack from a portion of the left wing of that army. He fell back stubbornly contesting the ground and giving time for the other divisions to withdraw. The retreat was conducted in good order. The British advanced in pursuit, having been reinforced by Lord Cornwallis with the Grenadiers and Light Infantry who had run all the way from the city. Generals Gray and Agnew led up their brigades in columns along the Main Street in pursuit. When the latter, at the head of his troops, reached the Mennonite Meeting House, he was mortally wounded by a shot from some one in ambush in the graveyard, and falling from his horse was carried to the rear. The pursuit was continued to Chestnut Hill and then given up. The British returned to the city and the American army to its former camping ground on the Perkiomen. The battle lasted from early dawn until after ten o'clock.

The loss of the Americans was as follows : Killed, officers, 30 ; men, 122. Wounded, officers, 117 ; men, 404. Prisoners, 400. Total, 1073.

Of the British : Killed, officers, 13 ; men 58. Wounded, officers, 55 ; men 395. Total, 521.

Colonel Matthews with the 9th Virginia Regiment of Greene's division became separated from their command and were captured in Mill Steeet near the Market Square. Many officers and men were slain in the attack upon the Chew House.   F. H.

FRANCIS DANIEL PASTORIUS

Prelude to the Pennsylvania Pilgrim.

I sing the Pilgrim of a softer clime
    And milder speech than those brave men's who brought
To the ice and iron of our winter time
    A will as firm, a creed as stern, and wrought
    With one mailed hand, and with the other fought.
Simply, as fits my theme, in homely rhyme
    I sing the blue-eyed German Spener taught,
Through whose veiled, mystic faith the Inward Light,
    Steady and still, an easy brightness, shone,
Transfiguring all things in its radiance white.
The garland which his meekness never sought
    I bring him ; over fields of harvest sown
    With seeds of blessing, now to ripeness grown,
I bid the sower pass before the reapers' sight.
                        JOHN G. WHITTIER.

THERE seems no proper place in the description of localities to mention Francis Daniel Pastorius, and any book of Germantown, even a guide book, would be incomplete without some allusion to him. He was born in Sommerhausen, Germany, September 26th, 1651. He reached Philadelphia August 6th, 1683. He first built a little house in Philadelphia,

HISTORIC GERMANTOWN

but later he moved to Germantown and became the leader, counsellor, lawyer, teacher and conveyancer for his countrymen. He was one of the best educated men in the colonies, being familiar with and writing fluently Greek, Latin, English, Dutch, German, Italian and French, He kept the records of the court, was bailiff of the borough, a justice of the peace and member of the Assembly, 1687 and 1691. He looked after the affairs of the Frankfort Company, the company owning the land comprised in Germantown, until 1700. He wrote a primer, which was the first original school book printed in Pennsylvania. Seven of his books were printed, besides which he left forty-three works in manuscript. It was he who wrote the protest against slavery which has been referred to at length elsewhere.

Pastorius married November 25th, 1688, Anna Klostermann, in Germantown, They were the parents of two sons, Johann Samuel, born March 30th, 1690, and Henry, born April 1st, 1692.

In 1698 Pastorius was master of the Friends School in Philadelphia and his home in Germantown stood idle. His home stood where now is the new Methodist Church, between Dr. Alexis Smith's house, No. 6019 Main Street, and Dr. Dunton's house, which originally stood where High Street is now opened through. Dr. Dunton tore the house down some thirty years ago and stones from it were used to build the rear portion of his present house, now No. 25 High Street. (See p. 94.)

Dr. Christopher Witt was Pastorius' neighbor and at one time they exchanged verses by throwing them over the fence to each other. They were both interested in flowers and horticulture and their verses related to these subjects.

Pastorius left a remarkable book called "The Beehive," a volume of family and miscellaneous matters containing a thousand pages of history, agriculture, philosophy, poetry, laws, etc., written in seven languages. The book is still in possession of the family, but is at present deposited in the Library of the University of Pennsylvania.

Whittier has immortalized Pastorius and the placid life of the early Germantown settlers in his "Pennsylvania Pilgrim."

Pastorius died February 27th, 1719. It is not known where he was buried, but it is supposed in the Friend's burial ground on the Main Street above Coulter.

Some of his descendants of the name Pastorius are still living in Germantown. For much other information concerning this talented and useful man see Judge Pennypacker's "Settlement of Germantown."

Bayard House

The streets of Germantown crossing or running off from the Main Street are here given for the convenience of the reader; also the number of the street, so that the places of interest described in the preceding pages may be readily located.

STREETS FROM WEST SIDE OF MAIN STREET	NORTH	STREETS FROM EAST SIDE OF MAIN STREET
Formerly Tullinger's Lane; now Carpenter Street	6900	Gorgas Street, formerly Gorgas Lane
	6800	Meehan Street Pleasant Street
Pelham Road Westview Phil-ellena Street	6700	Phil-ellena Street, formerly Church Street Springer Street
Franklin Street Formerly Good Street; now Sharpnack Street Weaver Street Upsal Street	6600	Sharpnack Street
	6500	Upsal Street Cliveden Avenue
Johnson Street Duval Street Washington Lane	6400	Johnson Street Duval Street
	6300	Washington Lane, formerly Abington Lane and Road
Tulpehocken Street	6200	Pastorius Street Herman Street
Walnut Lane Harvey Street Formerly Lafayette Street; now Haines Street	6100 6000	Walnut Lane, formerly Chestnut Street High Street Haines Street, formerly Methodist Lane, Bristol Lane, Pickius' Lane

Formerly Poor House Lane; now Rittenhouse Street	5900	Rittenhouse Street, formerly Centre Street
	5800	Price Street
Chelten Avenue	5700	Chelten Avenue
		Woodlawn Street
Maplewood Avenue	5600	Armat Street
Formerly Bensell's Lane, Ashmead's Lane; now School House Lane	5500	School House Lane
		Mill Street, formerly Church Lane, Luken's Mill Road
Coulter Street	5400	Coulter Street
Penn Street		Penn Street, formerly Shoemaker's Lane
Formerly Indian Queen Lane, Bowman's Lane; now Queen Street	5300	Bringhurst Street
	5200	Ashmead Street
		Collom Street, formerly Jefferson Street
Manheim Street	5100	Wister Street, formerly Duy's Lane, Dannehower's Mill Road
	5100	Garfield Street
Seymour Street	5000	Seymour Street, formerly Mehl Street
		East Clapier Street, formerly Mechlin Avenue
Logan Street	4900	Logan Street, east of Main Street formerly Fisher's Lane
Louden Street	4800	Wyoming Street
		Luray Street
Apsley Street		
Berkley Street	4600	Stenton Avenue
	SOUTH	

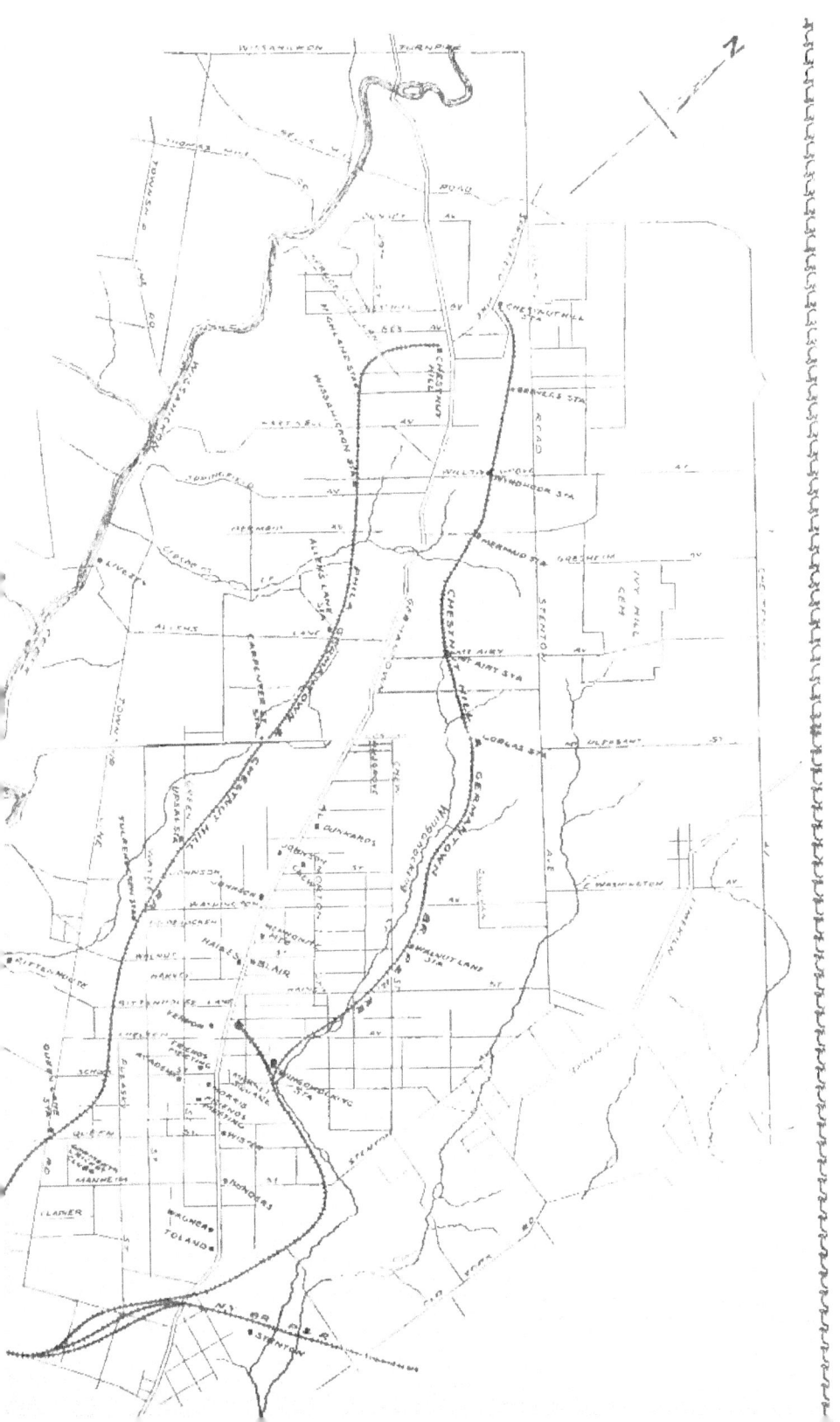

HISTORIC GERMANTOWN

INDEX

	PAGE		PAGE
Academy,	78	Fence, Revolutionary,	109
Alcott, Louisa M.,	58	Forrest, Colonel Thomas,	113, 140
Allen's House,	131	Friends' Meeting House,	57
Armat, Thomas,	35, 68		
Arrival of Immigrants,	17	Germantown, Battle of	153
Ashmeads,	59, 69	Germantown, Bibliography of	9
Awbry,	143	Germantown Cricket Club,	145
Ax's Burying Ground,	110	Germantown, How to Reach	14
		Germantown Library,	76
Bank of North America,	82	Germantown National Bank,	53, 76
Bank of Pennsylvania,	82	Germantown, Proposed Capitol U. S.,	144
Baptistry,	151	Germantown, Streets of	167
Barron, Commodore James,	42	Germantown Telegraph,	43
Beauregard, General P. G. T.,	132	Godfrey, Thomas,	138
Bibliography,	9	Gorgas Family,	131
Billmyer House,	122	Gowen House,	132
Branchtown,	137	Green Tree Tavern,	98
Butler Place,	134	Griffith House,	143
Buttonwood Tavern,	43		
		Hacker House,	46
Carlton,	146	Henry House,	37
Carriage Building,	60	Hesser House,	128
Charter Oak Library	110	Hill, Henry, Mansion,	146
Chew, Benjamin,	115	Hood's Burying Ground,	38
Chew House,	115		
Church of Brethren,	125	Jefferson, Thomas,	53
Clapier, Louis,	144	Johnson House,	106
Cliveden,	115		
Concord School,	110	Keipius, Johannes,	21
Cushman, Charlotte,	104	Kemble, Fanny,	134
		Keyser House,	105
Dallas, Alexander J.,	82	King of Prussia Tavern.	83
Drinker, Elizabeth,	77, 128	Kunders, Thones, House,	41
Dunkards,	125		
		Livezey House,	152
Engle House,	93	Logan, James,	33

173

HISTORIC GERMANTOWN

	PAGE
Log House,	132
Loudoun,	35
Lower Burying Ground,	38
Ludwig, Christopher,	90, 128, 140
Lutheran Church,	127
Lutheran Theological Seminary,	131
Market Square,	61
Market Square Church,	73
McKean Family,	144
Meade, General George G.,	132
Mehl House,	36
Mennonites,	18, 105
Methodist Church,	89
Middleton House,	140
Mifflin, Governor Thomas,	82
Monastery,	151
Morris House,	66
Morris-Littell House,	94
Mutual Fire Insurance Co.,	74
Neglee's Hill,	35
Ottinger House,	36
Paper Making, first in United States,	148
Pastorius, Francis Daniel,	17, 94, 162
Paul House,	128
Paxtang Boys,	62
Penn, William,	54, 70
Philadelphia National Cemetery,	140
Pomona,	113
Presbyterian Church,	84, 104
Price Homestead,	146
Randolph, Edmund,	53
Rittenhouse, David, birthplace	148
Robert's Mill,	138
Rock House,	54
Rodney House,	114
Roebuck Inn,	43

	PAGE
St. Luke's Church,	57
Sauer, Christopher,	49, 52, 127
Saving's Fund,	70
Shag Rag,	75
Ship House,	114
Shippen, Dr. William,	103
Slavery, Protest Against,	41
Sparrows, English,	121
Spencer House,	138
Spring Bank,	151
Stenton,	33
Stuart, Gilbert,	44
Toland House,	35
Town Hall,	90
Type First made in America,	50
United States Bank,	77
Unruh House,	131, 143
Upper Burying Ground,	110
Upsala,	121
Vernon Park,	87
Wagner House,	37
Wakefield Mills,	133
Warner Family,	97, 99
Washington, George,	44, 46, 53, 66, 74, 146
Washington, Martha,	139
Washington Tavern,	106
Wayne Junction,	33
White Cottage,	42
Whitfield, George,	75
Wister, Charles J.,	51
Wister, Owen,	45
Wister's, Sally, Journal,	51
Witherspoon, Major,	125
Witt, Dr. Christopher,	98, 99
Womens' Christian Association,	73
Wyck,	100
Zinzendorf, Count,	69, 74

www.ingramcontent.com/pod-product-compliance
Lightning Source LLC
Chambersburg PA
CBHW051102160426
43193CB00010B/1283